WHAT OTHERS ARE SAYING ABOUT *WORSHIP IS LIFE...*

"In *Worship Is Life,* Todd Marshall encourages the reader to answer the call to organize all of one's life around the God who made us, loves us, and gave his only Son as the model *par excellence* of a life completely submitted to worship. When we understand our worship as a response to the revelation of God with the purpose of conforming us to the lover of our souls, then we experience God's reconciling love and are sent forth into the world on mission with the fire of the Holy Spirit to spread God's love to the entire created order. There is nothing, absolutely nothing, more important than that! The author's ardor for God and his passion to see others adopt a lifestyle of self-emptying worship is contagious."

Dr. James R. Hart
President
Robert E. Webber Institute for Worship Studies

"Todd Marshall's book, *Worship Is Life*, is an in-depth philosophical look of living the daily worship life based on scriptural principles. Marshall writes, *"Works are essential because the revelation of God requires response"*… this is a story of a personal journey of faith and the response to the calling of a worship-full life."

Tom Matrone
Department chair and associate professor, director of Choral Studies
Music Department, Evangel University
Consultant to the Worship Resource & Consulting Department of the
Assemblies of God

D0802149

"*Worship Is Life* is a wonderful treatise on God's continual effort to bring us close to himself. Todd's easy-to-read investigation of the life of worship has the intensity of a pastor's heart who knows the dangers of idolatrous worship, and the understanding of one who is daily walking that same struggle. Chock-full of scripture and based on solid theology, this is a great book for worship/creative teams, pastors, and congregational members who are coming to terms with their own understanding of God's call to worship."

Dr. Dave Collins
North Central University

"Todd Marshall's new book, *Worship Is Life*, draws attention to the biblical pattern for Christian worship: revelation and response. Generally it seems that our current understanding of a corporate God encounter goes something like this: We get together. We ask him to come and join us. We sing some songs (new "hits" mostly). We listen to a sermon. We do a few other religious things. We go home. We come back next week and repeat. Todd suggests otherwise. God lovingly initiates, revealing himself (and ourselves) to us. We respond to him in dynamic love relationship. This relationship affects our entire lives. Todd goes on to describe the intense battle for true worship, offers strategies for worship service designers and leaders, and shares personal reflections from three decades of Christian leadership experience. Thank you, Todd, for writing this book."

David J. Pedde
Founding president / executive director
SANCTUS SCHOOL FOR WORSHIPERS

"Exodus 31 mentions a skilled craftsman who is filled with the Spirit to put on display God's work. Exodus 35 draws attention to skilled women, filled with the Spirit, who weave goat's hair together for the Master's use. Whether it is vocation as a craftsman or showcasing the divine camouflaged with the ordinary, Todd draws attention to the object and the heart of worship. I recommend this book and even more so recommend that your life as a craftsman or your life in the ordinary reflects the splendor of God's majesty."

Heath Adamson
National youth director
The General Council of the Assemblies of God

"Todd has written a powerful and thought-provoking book that should not only be read by worship pastors, but by all who call themselves Christians. He gives us a wonderful blend of personal insights and biblical theology to challenge our thinking of biblical worship. For those of us who know Todd, it is obvious that what he writes about he also lives."

Larry Bach
Dean
College of Fine Arts
North Central University

WORSHiP iS LiFE

FINDING OUR iDENTITY IN THE STORY OF WORSHIP

TODD MARSHALL

Unless otherwise specified, scripture quotations used in this book are taken from the Holy Bible, New International Version. Copyright 1973, 1978, 1984 by International Bible Society. Used by permission of Zondervan Publishing House. All rights reserved.

The "NIV" and "New International Version" trademarks are registered in the United States Patent and Trademark office by International Bible Society. Use of either trademark requires the permission of International Bible Society.

Scripture quotations marked "NKJV" are taken from The New King James Version / Thomas Nelson Publishers, Nashville: Thomas Nelson Publishers., Copyright 1982. Used by permission. All rights reserved.

ISBN: 978-1-4834-4471-0 (sc)
ISBN: 978-1-4834-4470-3 (e)

Library of Congress Control Number: 2016900261

Lulu Publishing Services rev. date: 04/18/2017

CONTENTS

Dedication ix

Foreword xi

Introduction xiii

Chapter 1   Worship Is Life 1

Chapter 2   The Battle for Our Worship 23

Chapter 3   Identity and Security 41

Chapter 4   Living a Life of Worship 57

Chapter 5   A Vision for Corporate Worship 81

Chapter 6   God's Provision 100

Acknowledgments 113

About the Author 115

Interested in hosting Worship is Life Ministry? 117

DEDICATION

*"He who finds a wife finds what is good
and receives favor from the LORD."*
Proverbs 18:22

To my wife, Brenda, a Proverbs 31 woman.
I love you and thank you for faithfully standing
with me as together we have discovered the
eternal truth that worship is life.

FOREWORD

Worship has always been a big part of my life. I have come to believe, in fact, that worship encompasses all of life. The first chapter of the Bible affirms that we are here on purpose. The last chapter affirms that Jesus is at the center of that purpose. What connects them all – purpose and Jesus – is a life of worship. Worship is more than the atmosphere of heaven. It is the heartbeat of God's people here on earth, our moment by moment response to a God who has graciously and clearly revealed himself to us.

I am just old enough to remember when three hymns and a chorus were pretty much standard fare for Sunday morning worship. It represented worship that was theological, testimonial, and musical – a response to God that, indeed, laid lasting foundations in my life. But as a young adult, I spiritually longed for more. It was the newly emerging praise and worship movement that would satisfy that hunger and introduce me to a whole new understanding of what worship could be. Worship became for me more than declarations *about* God, but the adoration *of* God. It was as if the post-service prayer ministry experiences that I was so accustomed to growing up were moving into the first part of church services, creating a holistic congregational worship "encounter."

Today, both declarational and adorational worship expressions are still woven into the spiritual fabric of my life. But after years of living and pastoring, I realized again that there was more. Beyond singing songs on Sundays or listening to worship music on our phones, worship is meant to permeate life itself. The Apostle Paul clues us in to this when, for example, he exhorts slaves (i.e., employees) not to go to work to serve a boss, but to serve and honor Christ himself (Ephesians 6:5). That is worship in its broadest sense. Everything we do, even our jobs, is because of him and can be for him. No wonder the powers of hell are aligned against the very idea of us living and loving that way.

Worship *is* life. That is what you will encounter in the pages of this book. Here Todd Marshall charts for us a wonderful journey into the heart of God for his glory and our transformation. I have known Todd personally for many years. He is an adept musician and skilled corporate worship leader. But he has also grown to understand worship in a very holistic and theologically robust way. May this book ignite a new fire in your own heart for responding to God's revelation of himself in a way that transforms identity, purpose, and life itself.

Dr. James Bradford
General Secretary of the Assemblies of God

INTRODUCTION

"There is nothing new under the sun."
Ecclesiastes 1:9

The book of Ecclesiastes states that there is nothing new under the sun. This timeless nugget of truth applies to biblical worship in many ways. So, how could there possibly be a need for another book about worship? I asked myself that question more times than I care to remember. Having read numerous books about worship, including devotional, historical, theological, and practical, I have barely scratched the surface regarding the wealth of books that have been written about worship by brilliant and passionate authors.

But consider this. While the sun is always shining, our view of the sun does not always reflect its true reality. Sometimes our view of the sun is hazy or intermittent as clouds float past. Other times our view of the sun is completely blocked out by dense fog or an overcast sky. Half of the time the sun is shining on the other side of the earth, and we are completely in the dark of night. My desire is that every reader could have the sun shine brighter on the *pattern*, the *purpose*, and the *pursuit* of biblical worship.

Biblical worship, God's description of worship, envelops all of one's life and permeates every moment of every day because God describes *worship* the same way he describes our *relationship* with him. Every person has a story. Every person is on a journey. Every person is in a life-and-death battle for his or her worship; his or her relationship with God. Many of us have been conditioned to look at this battle through the lens of good vs. evil or right vs. wrong. These are certainly manifestations, but at the core of biblical worship the battle is between worshiping God and worshiping self; between a God-focused relationship and a self-focused relationship.

Allow me to illustrate. Every moment we are alive, our physical heart is engaged. It is beating, working, and pumping blood through our veins. But a greater reality is that every moment we are alive, our spiritual heart is engaged.

Our spiritual heart is always in a posture of worshiping someone – God Almighty or our self. The moment by moment decision of who we bow our heart to is tied directly to where we find our identity. How we find our

a greater reality is that every moment we are alive, our spiritual heart is engaged

identity in God is told in the story of worship. When you consider what is at stake, and the fact that we are so conditioned to live for ourselves that we have difficulty recognizing it, the topic of worship cannot be overdone. Scripture reveals to us that worship is life because worship is relationship with God. It is not hyperbole to say that nothing matters more; for us and the people around us.

This book contains a healthy dose of biblical teaching and is illustrated with stories from my life: personal, family, and ministry. It is concise in that it reflects the core of the message, mission, and vision that the Lord has placed on our lives and in our hearts for the church and for the world. The God of the universe, who mysteriously exists as Spirit, Father, and Son, invites each one of us into a restored relationship with him through a life of worship!

CHAPTER 1

Worship Is Life

"Therefore, I urge you, brothers and sisters, in view of God's mercy, to offer your bodies as a living sacrifice, holy and pleasing to God – this is your spiritual (or reasonable) act of worship."
Romans 12:1

If you start to tell me a story, then you begin to get my attention. Introduce a conflict, add some suspense, mix in some mystery or romance, and now you have me hooked. Keep me intrigued about the outcome or, better yet, somehow relate it to me, and I will be back to hear more, repeatedly if necessary. Tell me the story is true, and the potential impact increases exponentially. Why are we so captivated by stories? How is it that in this age of technology that movies, television dramas, and written stories are more popular than ever? Speaking of technology, why do the countless stories accessible to us through social media and news outlets draw us in to the point of addiction? Could it be because Almighty God, our Creator, has fashioned us with a deep longing to identify with a story?

God is the author of the one true story. He invites us to identify *our* story with *his* story through a *life of worship.* He calls us to find our identity through a restored relationship with him and to partner in his mission to redeem the world. This relationship is made possible because of the complete work of Jesus, is made alive by the Holy Spirit of God, and is understood through the story of worship.

God is the author of the one true story

For thirty years, I have served the Lord by serving his church as a worship arts pastor. In the early years I simultaneously served as a youth pastor. Those were great years, and it was an honor to pour into the lives of those special young people. However, I must have blocked out some of those memories because whenever former youths share stories with me, my recollection is sketchy at best. It has become quite the running joke among us.

God has favored me with the blessing of living life and doing ministry in partnership with my amazing wife, Brenda. We met in the fall of 1983 at North Central Bible College in Minneapolis, MN (now North Central University) while being involved in the traveling chorale. She is a devoted woman of God, unconditionally supportive wife, compassionate and caring mother, gifted in the arts, and known for her velvety smooth alto voice.

Many life stories have helped shape my biblical understanding of "worship is life." However, none so dramatically as the one I am about to share. In the fall of 2000 we moved to Smithtown, New York (Long Island), to serve the congregation of Smithtown Gospel Tabernacle. At the time our daughter, Kelsie, was nine, and our son, Taylor, was two and a half. We served there for almost fourteen years, but during the final eighteen months or so, I was experiencing what one could describe as a shifting in the desires of my heart. The activities of ministry that once brought life were now draining me, and former desires were being replaced with a growing desire to minister in other ways. I have learned over the years to recognize this shifting as the Spirit of God guiding me (Psalm 37:4).

During this season the shifting came to a head, propelling me into an intense time of seeking the Lord and being deeply attentive to his voice. Over a seventy-two-hour period, I heard the Spirit of God speak to me on

I have learned over the years to recognize this shifting as the Spirit of God guiding me

three different occasions. His voice was extremely clear, and the messages were more distinct than at any other time in my life. It was the kind of clarity that went beyond the category of God-inspired thoughts, where the best description is as if God interrupted my thoughts with his thoughts. I can only surmise that he graciously offered this clarity knowing my need to hear his words in order to respond with true faith.

The first message came on Sunday morning of Mother's Day 2013. I was in the sanctuary before the first of our three services and walking up the stairs to the balcony where our technology booth was located. At the time, no one else was in the sanctuary, but I heard the Spirit of God interrupt my thoughts with these words: "You've done what you can do here." I was simply stunned by the abruptness and simplicity of the words. My immediate reply was, "Wow! Really, Lord? Okay ... but could you give me a little more to go on here?" All throughout the day's services I was doing my best to listen and look for any sign or clue that would confirm or elaborate on what I had heard.

The next morning I knelt in my traditional place of daily waiting on the Lord, trying to listen and discern. Nothing. After an hour or so I headed upstairs. While getting ready to go to the office, my thoughts were again interrupted and I heard God say, "I have called you to serve me by serving my church, especially in the area of worship. All that I have poured into you, you have poured out here, and it has become part of their DNA, and I need you to give it someplace else."

Now, this was getting serious. Naturally, I was sharing these messages with Brenda, and we were both trying to refrain from freaking out. We continued to pray together, trusting and asking the Lord to make his way clear.

Tuesday brought no further word. Then on Wednesday, May 15, 2013, the word of the Lord came to me during my early morning time with him, saying, "I've given you a message for my church concerning worship, and I am positioning you so this message will have a greater influence." That was it. I told Brenda, and she cried. A few days later we told Taylor, and we all cried. While Brenda and I had spent nearly half of our married lives here, Taylor had grown up here. We talked about how difficult it was going to be to leave friends, familiarity, and potential opportunities. But we also talked about the fact that while the Lord specifically spoke to me, he had all of us in mind, and his promises to take care of us were true, both as a family and as individuals. Our part was to be obedient servants and trust his words.

Kelsie was still in Minneapolis, where she had just graduated from North Central University, our alma mater. She was spending a few extra weeks with her fiancé, Ben, before coming home to make final preparations for a June 29 wedding. We had been keeping them posted, and they were as stunned as we were.

On Thursday of that week, I shared with our pastor what had transpired. He was gracious and supportive. Over the next two days, I proceeded to sit down with each of the other eight pastors and share with them. Even though at the time there was no sign of a plan moving forward, some of the elders felt it would be better to inform the congregation sooner rather than later. Another staff pastor was announcing his resignation, and they decided to inform the congregation of both on the same day. Over the next two weeks, I called all my ministry leaders and close friends. I shared with our choir, orchestra, and other team members. On Sunday, June 2, we shared with the congregation in all three services. These weeks were filled with surprise and sadness for everyone. At first, informing everyone early in the process seemed premature. But one significant blessing that came from this was that during Kelsie's wedding, no secrets were being kept, and her good-byes could be freely and lovingly shared.

Our pastor graciously agreed that we would move forward trusting the Lord to reveal the next steps. We envisioned three possible scenarios: an opportunity would present itself that fulfilled the word I had received, another word would come indicating to just pack up and go, or the church would find a replacement for us, necessitating our stepping out and leaving. We proceeded through the summer and early fall with no indications. Then, in October, the executive pastor came across a potential candidate for our replacement. As the process unfolded, it became clear that this was indeed the candidate. On the first Sunday in December, the church membership voted him in as the next worship arts pastor. He shadowed me during our Christmas presentations and trained under me during January. On Saturday, February 1, with the help of about forty friends, we loaded the trucks. That was just one of many days we felt the love and support of our church family and was a beautiful picture of the Body of Christ even in the midst of the sadness of saying good-bye. At 6:00 a.m. on Sunday, February 2, 2014, we left Long Island and headed to Minnesota. So what does this story have to do with worship?

Worship is life; what is it? 'Worship is Life' is connecting our relationship with God to our relationship with life. When we hear the word *worship*, many think of a corporate gathering for a service designed to give honor to God. Some may think of a portion of the service such as singing songs. While these thoughts are true, there is a great danger to this narrow view of worship. An unintended consequence of our contemporary language of worship is that it runs the risk of promoting a critical struggle that mankind has faced since that first fateful step of independence – a disconnect between our relationship with God and our relationship with life. Instead of looking at worship through the lens of a church service or through the lens of music, scripture teaches us to look at life through the lens of

there is a great danger to this narrow view of worship

worship; worship is life! We find this life of worship through God's story.

While we cannot prove his story in the same way one would prove something in a court of law or a science lab, we can know God's story is true. We can know it is true because God reveals himself to us. He has revealed who he is, what he has done, and what we are to do. He has revealed himself through his Word and by his Spirit as: Creator, Provider, Protector, Defender, Healer, Father, Friend, Savior, Redeemer, Risen Lord, Intercessor, Soon Coming King, Victorious Warrior, Helper, Counselor, Comforter, Guide, Teacher, Empowerer, and the list goes on. These names reflect how God Almighty has sovereignly chosen to reveal himself as Father, Son, and Holy Spirit of God. Our response to the revelation of God is what he calls worship (relationship). The pattern of biblical worship is: God reveals, and we respond.[1] This is 'Worship is Life'.

The pattern of biblical worship is: God reveals, and we respond

Worship is life; why does it matter? As we begin to examine this perspective more closely, I am going to highlight two aspects of God's nature which we seldom speak about: God

---

[1] I first began to study the biblical pattern of revelation and response as a result of a teaching given by Ross Parsley at a worship conference in Texas.

creates systems, and he works in patterns. Creation functions through systems: solar systems, ecosystems, weather systems, etc. Our bodies function through systems: circulatory system, nervous system, skeletal system, reproductive system, etc. The scriptures are full of patterns established by God: Sabbath day every seven days, Sabbath year every seven years, seasonal festivals, sowing and reaping, repentance and forgiveness, obedience and blessing, etc.

We see this evidenced in us because *we* create systems and *we* work in patterns. This is not surprising as we are made in the image of God! Now watch this. God has created a system for growing his kingdom. His *system* for growing his kingdom is that he works through those who are a part of his kingdom! In other words, when we give a favorable response to the revelation of God then we enter into relationship with him. We then become the ones who work with God to bring others into relationship with him. This speaks to the purpose of worship which we will look at more closely in chapters 4 and 5. This system works by a *pattern* set forth by God which is *revelation* and *response*. This is how God does relationship, how he describes worship, and how he grows his kingdom.

It is true that God inhabits the praises of his people (Psalm 22:3), but we are not the initiators. God initiates by revealing himself, and invites us to respond. In fact, God is not just the subject of our worship; he is thoroughly involved in our offering of worship. God reveals who he is and what he's done; Jesus as our High Priest offers our worship as a mediator, and the Holy Spirit of God breathes upon and inspires our worship. While our role is significant, after all it is a relationship, it pales in comparison to the role God plays. We know this relationship is not centered on us, but we continue to battle our tendency to make it about us. We will thoroughly address this battle in chapter 2.

Since worship is life, then what exactly is worship? The Bible doesn't give us a chapter and verse definition of worship. That should not be surprising to us because the Bible is not a dictionary. The Bible is the story of God revealing himself to us. Instead, the Bible shows us this pattern by giving us pictures of worship, descriptions of worship, and original language words that we translate into the word '*worship*'. Let's begin by looking at two Greek words in the New Testament.

The first word is *proskuneo*, which literally means to bow, to show reverence and adoration. The second word is *letreuo*, which means service, obedient service. When you look at these two words together, you see a much bigger picture than an occasional physical bowing down. You see a mind-set, an attitude, and a life being lived in the posture of bowing before the Lord. When a faithful servant physically bows before his master, it is an outward manifestation of an inner attitude being carried out each day. Therefore, if we were to express a sound biblical definition of worship, it would be: God reveals who he is, what he has done, and what we are to do, and we respond by living a life of obedient service in reverence and adoration. I have included a visual of a three-legged stool to illustrate the three aspects of revelation and response. All three legs work together to hold up God's description and pattern for worship.

This pattern is seen all through the scriptures. Sometimes you can see it in a single verse such as Psalm 63:3: "Because your love is better than life, my lips will praise you." The revelation is that God's love is better than life, and the response is we will praise him with our mouth.[2] Other times you see the pattern in an entire book. The book of Romans is an amazing example of this, as we will begin to see in this chapter and continue in chapter 4. Many scriptures help paint this complete picture of worship, and in a moment we will examine two verses in particular, Romans 12:1 and Matthew 4:10.

---

[2] In Psalm 63:3, the Hebrew word for praise is *shabach*, which means to shout.

Looking closely at chapters 1 through 8 of Romans, we see how the apostle Paul points to the revelation by presenting the full story of God, and what a story it is! In chapter 1, Paul starts at the beginning of the story by speaking of creation. On the day the Spirit of God breathed life into Adam, everything changed! Man became a living being and God invited him into relationship. The revelation of creation is so powerful that Paul declares in verse 20 that for this reason man is without excuse. He then takes chapters 1 through 3 to tell the next part of the story, the fall of man. The day that Adam and Eve took that first fateful step of independence, everything changed! The power of sin to bring death was released into humanity and throughout the world.

Paul takes a full five chapters, 3 through 7, to tell the next part of the story; redemption through Christ for all people. The day Christ died on the cross, everything changed! The power of sin to bring eternal death was broken! But, thank God that is not the end of the story, and in chapters 6 and 7 Paul continues the story with Christ's resurrection. The day Christ rose from the dead, everything changed! The power of death itself was broken and the promise of eternal life was released!

In the first part of chapter 8, Paul lays out the next part of the story which is life in the Spirit. This is the part of the story we are living in right now because on the day of Pentecost, everything changed! Instead of God breathing his Spirit on certain individuals at certain times, every person who responds favorably to the revelation of God becomes

12

the dwelling place of the Spirit of God! Paul concludes the story in the last part of chapter 8 with Christ's return and our future glory. On the day Christ returns, everything will change again! No mind can imagine what God has in store!

As Paul prepares to transition from revelation to response, he takes chapters 9 through 11 to share his heart for the Jews and his call to the gentiles. Chapter 11 then culminates with Paul's personal response as he pens one of the great doxologies of praise to our God (Romans 11:33–36):

> Oh, the depth of the riches and the knowledge of God! How unsearchable his judgments, and his paths beyond tracing out! "Who has known the mind of the LORD? Or who has been his counselor?" "Who has ever given to God, that God should repay him?" For from him and through him and to him are all things. To him be glory forever! Amen.

Through these eleven chapters, Paul has shown who God has revealed himself to be and what he has done. In Romans 12:1, Paul declares what our response should be to such a revelation by stating, "Therefore, I urge you, brothers and sisters, in view of God's mercy, to offer your bodies as a living sacrifice, holy and pleasing to God – this is your true and proper worship."

Paul is inferring that we no longer kill animals and offer dead bodies as sacrifices to God. We now offer our whole selves as living sacrifices; worship is life. The Greek word for worship in this verse is *letreia*, which is derived from the word *letreuo*, meaning obedient service. When we examine this verse in various translations, the word *worship* is found in some translations and the word *service* is found in others. One translation uses both words! So why is there such difficulty in agreeing on which word to use, and why is it important? It is because you cannot separate worship from life. Worship is not an isolated event such as offering a sacrifice, but is all encompassing; worship is life! The entire book of Romans is a beautiful example of the biblical pattern of worship – revelation and then response. Paul gives us a practical breakdown of our response from Romans 12:2

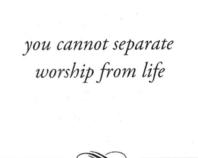

you cannot separate worship from life

through chapter 15. We will look at this more closely in chapter 4.

Matthew 4:10 reads: "Jesus said to him, 'Away from me, Satan! For it is written: "Worship the LORD your God, and serve him only."' This is Jesus' response to Lucifer's third temptation, which we will look at more in depth in chapters 2 and 3. We should not be surprised that Jesus, who intimately understands the battle for worship, rebukes the enemy by using both words for worship in one statement, "Worship (*proskuneo*) the LORD your God and serve (*letreuo*) him only." Worship is life!

The Old Testament has numerous examples of individuals living out lives of biblical worship. The account of Abraham is certainly one example worthy of our attention. The story begins in Genesis chapter 12 with the call of Abraham: "The LORD had said to Abram, 'Leave your country, your people and your father's household and go to the land I will show you. I will make you into a great nation and I will bless you; I will make your name great, and you will be a blessing'" (Genesis 12:1–2).

Immediately we see the two dynamics that shape biblical worship. First, God reveals himself to Abraham, and in this instance it was by speaking to him. God is always the initiator, and he initiates by revealing himself. Our response to his revelation is worship. In this case, Abraham responded in obedience by packing up his family and belongings and heading to "the land I will show you." Second, God calls

Where we find our identity and place our security is at the heart of worship

Abraham in a way that confronts identity and security: "leave your country, your people and your father's household." Where we find our identity and place our security is at the heart of worship, and we will unpack this further in chapter 3.

While scripture does not record the first seventy-five years of Abraham's life, we do see a good deal of the last one hundred years of his life. Yes, there were bumps along the way when Abraham's actions were found wanting, but by and large we witness a worshipful life being lived out in obedience to God's word of revelation. Abraham's life of worship also was marked with moments of ritual worship. Twice on his journey he builds an altar to the Lord, recorded in verse seven and again in verse eight of chapter 12. But these events are like mile markers on a journey of a worshipful life expressed in obedient service. This is made abundantly clear when the word of God came to Abraham and instructed him to offer his son Isaac as a sacrifice. "Then God said, 'Take your son, your only son, Isaac, whom you love, and go to the region of Moriah. Sacrifice him there as a burnt offering on one of the mountains I will tell you about'" (Genesis 22:2).

Much has been said and written concerning this stunning test that the Lord gives to Abraham. Not only is Isaac his son, he is the fulfillment of the promise made to Abraham that began this whole journey in the first place. The truth I want to keep emphasizing is that Abraham lived a life of worship by bowing his life before the Lord in trusting obedience. In verse five of Genesis chapter 22, Abraham says to his servants, "Stay here with the donkey while I and the boy go over there. We will worship and then we will come back to you." This verse again demonstrates Abraham's trust and confidence in the Lord and reveals how this kind of living is tied directly to an attitude of worship (relationship with God). While we see relationship with God from the very beginning of Genesis, this happens to be the first verse in the Bible where we find the word 'worship'.

The Hebrew word for worship in this verse is *histahawa*, which, like other Hebrew words for worship as well as the Greek word *proskuneo*, means to bow down, fall down, do reverence, worship. Abraham is not just going to Mount Moriah for an isolated worship event to offer up a great sacrifice. His physical act of bowing down at this altar of sacrifice is a manifestation of his life bowed down in worship. We see this biblical principle of worship lived out in the Old Testament in the lives of Noah, Joseph, Moses, Samuel, David, Daniel, and so many others. We see it again in the New Testament in the lives of Mary, Joseph, the disciples, Paul, and others. God reveals himself to each one of them, and in turn they respond by bowing their lives in obedient service. Jesus is the ultimate revelation of God, which is

Jesus, the Revealer, allowed himself to become the greatest example of a life bowed down in obedient service

why it is beyond comprehension that "he made himself nothing by taking the very nature of a servant, being made in human likeness. And being found in appearance as a man, he humbled himself by becoming obedient to death – even death on a cross!" (Philippians 2:7–8). Jesus, the Revealer, allowed himself to become the greatest example of a life bowed down in obedient service.

This is precisely what our story at the beginning of this chapter has to do with worship. Biblical worship is living a life that is bowed before the Lord in obedience with adoration and reverence. Brenda and I have heard many times from others that we have stepped out and are living by faith. If it is understood that living by faith is hearing the revelation of God's word and responding by stepping out in obedience to that word then yes, we are living by faith. Faith comes by hearing the word of God (Romans 10:17). This verse that is foundational to our relationship with God is another demonstration of biblical worship. God reveals himself through his word and we respond out of obedience by faith – trust and confidence in his word. When Peter stepped out of the boat to walk on the water, he was not presuming upon Jesus or taking a calculated risk. He was responding to Jesus revealing himself and saying, "Come" (Matthew 14:25–29).

If stepping out and living by faith is referring to leaving behind a regular paycheck, housing, and many other "fringe" benefits that come from being on staff at a large church, for a life of "completely trusting the Lord" for our provision, then the point has been missed. Every person on earth is completely dependent upon the Lord for his or her provisions. Circumstances cause us to become aware of that dependence with varying levels of intensity. Many take the Lord completely out of the equation and view their provision as being solely dependent on their own ability, skill, building a business, or securing a job. Others acknowledge a dependency on God, and yet feelings of security are threatened when a job is lost. Small business owners, farmers, missionaries, itinerant ministers like ourselves, all have days of waking up and wondering where the provision is coming from. But in reality, we are all in the same place of depending on God whether we realize it or not. Living by faith, confidently trusting regardless of the circumstances, is living out the biblical description of worship: God reveals himself, and we respond in obedience with adoration and reverence. God calls this worship. He calls this relationship.

Whether you are reading the story of Abraham leaving his home, us leaving Long Island, or navigating your own journey, living a life of worship is about more than just those "big" moments in life. "Worship is life" is a mind-set, an attitude, an approach to life that permeates each moment of every day. If you think this sounds hard, it is. If you think it sounds impossible, think again. If you are wondering

"Worship is life" is a mind-set, an attitude, an approach to life that permeates each moment of every day

how it could possibly be worth it, remind yourself who God has revealed himself to be and how he strengthens us by his grace to worship him with our lives in relationship with him. Worship is life!

KEY POINTS

1. God describes worship the same way he describes relationship. He reveals himself to us and invites us to respond. He invites us into relationship with him through a life of worship.

2. God has created a system for growing his kingdom. His system is that he works through those who are a part of his kingdom. God works through a pattern to activate his system; this pattern is revelation and response.

3. God reveals who he is through his nature, and invites us to respond with reverence. He reveals what he has done through his story, and invites us to respond with adoration. He reveals what we are to do through his words, and invites us to respond with obedience.

DISCUSSION QUESTIONS

1. Considering God's pattern of revelation and response, list the similarities between the worship of God, and a relationship with God. (Genesis 12:1, 2; Matthew 4:10; Romans 12:1; Acts 17:28)

2. What are some ways you recognize that God has worked through you? How does God working in this way grow his kingdom? What other ways might God could work through you and what part do you play? (Galatians 5:22, 23; 1 Corinthians 12:7–11)

3. Explain how you could be more attentive to God's nature, story, and words? (Psalm 16:5; 33:18; Isaiah 42:5–8; Romans 1:20)

NOTES

CHAPTER 2

The Battle for Our Worship

*"I am the LORD; that is my name! I will not give
my glory to another or my praise to idols."*
Isaiah 42:8

There is nothing in all of life that is more significant than
our relationship with God. It is so simple, but it is not easy.
It is not complicated, but at times it can be so hard. How
does the joy of a relationship with God sometimes feel like a
burden of religious ritual or failure on our part? It is because
we are in a battle for our relationship with God; a battle
for our worship. Battles are not pleasant. Battles are messy;
battles are ugly, and, worst of all, people die in battle. Every
person is in a battle of life and death for his or her worship.

The scriptures show us the pattern for worship: God reveals
himself, and we respond. Our response to the revelation of
God can be favorable or unfavorable. We can have a favorable
response to the revelation of God by bowing our lives to

him (accepting relationship), or we can have an unfavorable response to the revelation of God by bowing our lives to an idol – to be blunt, our selves (rejecting relationship). I first talked about this in the introduction. Our spiritual heart is in a constant posture of worship. We worship God, or we worship the idol of self. But God will not give his praise to idols. He pursues us relentlessly. So like it or not, we are in this battle.

We all have this in common: the idol of self. Anything else we would identify as an idol is simply an expression of appeasing the idol of self. For years I have wrestled with knocking over certain expressions of self-idolatry in my life. One of these has been sports. I was raised in a family that placed a high value on sports and athleticism. Growing up, we participated in sports by playing, coaching, watching live or on television, listening on the radio, and cheering for family members and our favorite players and teams. This high level of interest in sports carried over into my adult life. I continued playing, watching, listening, and cheering. The love of sports is widely accepted in our country and around the world. The fact that sports was my favorite hobby would be of little concern to most.

While there are some life lessons that can be learned by being involved in sports, the more I studied biblical worship throughout my ministry years, the more I began to recognize that the dominant attitudes of sports were at odds with the attitude of worship. Biblical worship requires a selfless attitude that expresses complete dependence on God and results in laying your life down for God and for others. Sports, I am sorry to admit, brings out attitudes primarily focused on self. When I win I feel good, and when I lose I feel bad (the thrill of victory and the agony of defeat). However, I can feel good if I am part of a losing team, but I performed well (How pathetic is that?), yet I am angry with myself if I don't perform well, even if the team wins. When I cheer for an individual or a team, it is rooted in self-interest. I associate with an individual through a personal relationship or a personal interest. I associate with a team through my connection to a community such as a school, town, state, or country. When my team loses, I am disappointed and often angry at them or at an individual who cost the team the game. When they win, I am elated, and I boast about it. I have negative feelings for the competition. The list can go on, but there is one obvious common denominator: self. This attitude toward sports sounds a bit fanatical, which, of course, is where we get the term *fan*. I find it fascinating that the word *fanatic* is from the Latin word *fanaticus*, meaning excessive enthusiasm, and is derived from the word *fanum*, meaning temple. We have just described a fan as someone who is worshiping at a temple with excessive enthusiasm. No matter what or who we are fans of; it is just one expression of idolatry that flows out of our one true idol: self.

The revelation that the real idol is self is critical to understanding the battle for our worship. When we think about idolatry, we typically think about objects that we give too much time and attention such as a person, possessions, hobby, career, addiction, or habit. In reality, these are only expressions of the one true idol: our self. We are all unique individuals, and so the expressions of self-idolatry will be different for each of us. There are certain trigger points that we all have in common: hunger, thirst, discomfort, pain, sickness, and death. Whether the trigger points are common to all or are our own, for all of us it boils down to the idol of self; and God will not share his glory or give his praise to idols. There is a battle for our worship. Will we worship God or worship self? This battle of self-worship is not confined to materialistic societies but is universal. Whether someone is a first world consumerist, a third world survivalist, or a jungle tribalist, the battle of self-worship is universal because it is rooted in identity and

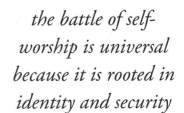

the battle of self-worship is universal because it is rooted in identity and security

security, which will be the focus of chapter 3. For now we will focus on the part of God's story that tells us where this battle began. When you are in a battle, you need to know your enemy – his scheme and his tactics. So we will now look at three pictures: Lucifer in the throne room with God, Lucifer in the garden with Eve, and Lucifer in the wilderness with Jesus.

To understand the beginning of the story, we must turn to the middle of the Bible, where we find two prophecies that contain descriptions of Lucifer, or Satan, commonly referred to as the devil. Lucifer plays a key role in God's story. While some may shy away from speaking about our adversary, scripture affirms that "we are not unaware of his schemes" (2 Corinthians 2:11). Before revealing his greatest scheme, and his greatest desire, I want to first focus specifically on how he was created, where he was positioned, and what purpose he served. These are the three things we all have in common with Lucifer: a God-given design, a God-given position, and a God-given purpose.

The first description of Lucifer is found in a prophecy against the king of Babylon in Isaiah 14:12–15 (NKJV):

> "How you are fallen from heaven, O Lucifer, son of the morning! How you are cut down to the ground, You who weakened the nations! For you have said in your heart: 'I will ascend into heaven, I will exalt my throne above the stars of God; I will also sit on the mount of the congregation on the farthest sides of the north; I will ascend above the heights of the clouds, I will be like the Most High.' Yet you shall be brought down to Sheol, to the lowest depths of the Pit."

The second description is found in a prophecy against the king of Tyre in Ezekiel 28:11–17 (NKJV):

Moreover the word of the LORD came to me, saying, "Son of man, take up a lamentation for the king of Tyre, and say to him, 'Thus says the LORD God: "You were the seal of perfection, full of wisdom and perfect in beauty. You were in Eden, the garden of God; every precious stone was your covering: the sardius, topaz, and diamond, beryl, onyx, and jasper, sapphire, turquoise, and emerald with gold. The workmanship of your timbrels and pipes was prepared for you on the day you were created. You were the anointed cherub who covers; I established you; you were on the holy mountain of God; You walked back and forth in the midst of the fiery stones. You were perfect in your ways from the day you were created, till iniquity was found in you. By the abundance of your trading you became filled with violence within, and you sinned; therefore I cast you as a profane thing out of the mountain of God; and I destroyed you, O covering cherub, from the midst of the fiery stones. Your heart was lifted up because of your beauty; you corrupted your wisdom for the sake of your splendor; I cast you to the ground, I laid you before Kings, that they might gaze at you."

Before making key observations in these two passages, let me address why I attribute these descriptions to Lucifer. Many scholars agree with the classic interpretation that these portions of scripture represent a dual purpose of rebuking these two kings and describing Lucifer. Some disagree, so I will refer to several reasons I am confident these passages apply to Lucifer as well as the kings to which they are directed. First, there are portions of these descriptions that could not possibly apply to any human being. For example, "you were the anointed cherub who covers." Second, Lucifer rules the nations (god of this age, 2 Corinthians 4:4; ruler of the kingdom of the air, Ephesians 2:2; undisputed by Jesus during the temptations, Matthew 4:8–10), and the prophets are describing the prideful being behind two particularly prideful rulers of nations, the king of Babylon and the king of Tyre. Third, Jesus "saw Satan fall like lightning from heaven" (Luke 10:18), and it is reasonable to conclude these scriptures describe that event.

Fourth, in the verses preceding Luke 10:18 where Jesus says he saw Satan fall from heaven, Jesus makes references to both the Ezekiel and Isaiah passages. Luke 10:13–14 reads: "Woe to you, Chorazin! Woe to you, Bethsaida! For if the miracles that were performed in you had been performed in Tyre and Sidon, they would have repented long ago, sitting in sackcloth and ashes. But it will be more bearable for Tyre and Sidon at the judgment than for you." Twice, Jesus references Tyre and Sidon just before saying he saw Satan fall from heaven. The Ezekiel description of Lucifer in the prophecy against the king of Tyre is immediately followed by a prophecy against the king of Sidon.

Now, let's compare Luke 10:15 with Isaiah 14:14–15. Looking at Luke 10:15, we read: "And you, Capernaum, will you be lifted to the heavens? No, you will go down to Hades." In Isaiah 14:14–15 we read: "'I will ascend above the heights of the clouds, I will be like the Most High.' Yet you shall be brought down to Sheol, to the lowest depths of the Pit." Jesus echoes the same language used in the Isaiah description of Lucifer. I cannot imagine that it is unintentional or coincidental that Jesus, and Luke (under the inspiration of the Holy Spirit), make such a strong connection between the passage where Jesus saw Satan fall from heaven and these two descriptions of Lucifer in the Old Testament.

Fifth, concerning an overseer, Paul writes in 1 Timothy 3:6: "He must not be a recent convert, or he may become conceited and fall under the same judgment as the devil." Paul directly connects the sin of conceit to the judgment that Lucifer came under. It seems quite reasonable, if not obvious, that Paul was drawing from these same Old Testament descriptions. Without attributing these descriptions to Lucifer, we would have little else to turn to regarding the background of the enemy of our souls.

Now let us consider a few key observations. The Ezekiel description refers to "the anointed cherub who covers" and "covering cherub." To gain some insight into what is meant by a covering cherub, we turn to the book of Exodus where God is giving Moses instructions for constructing the tabernacle and its furnishings. A covering cherub is directly linked to the most significant furnishing, which is the Ark of the Covenant representing the presence of God. The description is found in Exodus 25:10–22:

> "Have them make an ark of acacia wood – two and a half cubits long, a cubit and a half wide, and a cubit and a half high. Overlay it with pure gold, both inside and out, and make a gold molding around it. Cast four gold rings for it and fasten them to its four feet, with two rings on one side and two rings on the other. Then make poles of acacia wood and overlay them with gold. Insert the poles into the rings on the sides of the ark to carry it. The poles are to remain in the rings of this ark; they are not to be removed. Then put in the ark the tablets of the covenant law, which I will give you. "Make an atonement cover of pure gold – two and a half cubits long and a cubit and a half wide. And make two cherubim out of hammered gold at the ends of the cover. Make one cherub

on one end and the second cherub on the other; make the cherubim of one piece with the cover, at the two ends. The cherubim are to have their wings spread upward, overshadowing the cover with them. The cherubim are to face each other, looking toward the cover. Place the cover on top of the ark and put in the ark the tablets of the covenant law that I will give you. There, above the cover between the two cherubim that are over the ark of the Testimony, I will meet with you and give you all my commands for the Israelites."

The lid of the Ark is called the atonement cover, or mercy seat, and this is where God said he would meet with Moses and give him all the commands for the Israelites. On either end is an angel, or cherub, with its wings spread out "covering" the Ark, the presence of God. This gives us insight into how God positioned Lucifer in heaven and the purpose he served; covering the presence of God as a covering cherub, or guardian cherub.

Keeping in mind the position and purpose God gave to Lucifer, we turn our attention to how God designed him. The Ezekiel passage records that "every precious stone was your covering" and goes on to list the stones. When are precious stones most brilliant? It is when light is reflecting off of them. We begin to see a stunning image when we picture the light of the glory of God emanating forth and reflecting off the precious stones that were covering Lucifer causing him to perhaps be the most brilliant creature in heaven. This was nothing out of Lucifer's own doing but because of how God designed him and positioned him.

The same passage then says, "The workmanship of your timbrels and pipes was prepared for you on the day you were created." The description refrains from telling us how timbrels and pipes were integrated into his creation, but it is clearly stated they were for him. Now, picture the breath of the presence of God blowing through these pipes filling the atmosphere of heaven with the most beautiful sound. Lucifer is brilliant in appearance and beautiful in sound. None of this was his own doing but entirely the result of how God made him and where God positioned him. However, Lucifer's heart became "lifted up," and he desired to "be like the Most High," so God cast him out of heaven. Here we see our first glimpse of Lucifer's greatest desire: to be worshiped.[1]

Lucifer's name literally means morning star or light bearer. This makes complete sense when we see how he was designed and positioned. No wonder scripture says he "masquerades as an angel of light" (2 Corinthians 11:14). The Hebrew

---

[1] I cannot recall when I first started studying the connection between the battle for our worship and the fall of Lucifer. However, I heard about the imagery of the reflection of God's glory and the breath of God in a session at Pure Worship Institute at North Central University, where Heath Adamson shared a vision he had received from the Lord.

word for Lucifer is *heylel*, which is derived from the word *halal*. *Halal* means "to praise" and is the primary word for praise in the Old Testament. Of course, this is where we get the word *hallelujah*, meaning "praise God." We begin to see the connection between Lucifer and praise and why there is indeed a battle for our worship.

To pick up the story we turn to Genesis 3:5, where we find Lucifer tempting Eve to eat from the tree of the knowledge of good and evil. Lucifer says to Eve, "For God knows that when you eat from it your eyes will be opened, and you will be like God, knowing good and evil." In essence, Lucifer was saying, "Eve, you can be like God. You can be your own God. You … can … worship … yourself. You can do things your way instead of God's way. You can have things your way instead of God's way." Lucifer's greatest scheme is to tempt us to worship ourselves instead of God. Sin is rebellion against God with self at the center. Here is the battle for our worship.

In the previous paragraph we examined the exchange in the garden between Lucifer and Eve (we'll get to Adam later) but now we jump ahead four thousand years in the story and find Lucifer, or Satan, in the wilderness with Jesus. After Jesus is baptized by John in the Jordan River, the Holy Spirit descends upon Jesus like a dove, and the Father declares his love and pleasure with him (Matthew 3:13–17). In Matthew chapter 4, we find that the Holy Spirit has led Jesus into the wilderness to be tempted by the devil. Jesus fasted forty days and nights and was hungry. Satan comes to Jesus and says in verse 3, "If you are the Son of God, tell these stones to become bread." Satan tempts Jesus with the same scheme he used on Eve. Jesus, you can worship yourself. You can take your own power and your own ability to meet your needs and fill your own desires. Jesus immediately pulls out the Sword of the Spirit and quotes Deuteronomy 8:3b: "Man does not live on bread alone but on every word that comes from the mouth of the LORD."

After being soundly rebuked by Jesus, Satan takes him to the highest point of the temple and tries to give him a taste of his own medicine by using scripture: "If you are the Son of God," he said, "throw yourself down. For it is written: 'He will command his angels concerning you, and they will lift you up in their hands, so that you will not strike your foot against a stone'" (Matthew 4:6). Satan's scheme never changes: "Jesus, you can worship yourself. You can take an act of your own will and prove your identity." Jesus again rebukes him by quoting Deuteronomy 6:16a: "Do not test the LORD your God." Then we come to the third temptation, and Satan clearly shows his greatest desire when we pick up the story in Matthew 4:8–9: "Again, the devil took him to a very high mountain and showed him all the kingdoms of the world and their splendor. 'All this I will give you,' he said, 'if you will bow down and worship me.'" In other words: "Jesus, you can have it all if you will just … bow … down … and worship me." Satan's greatest desire is to be worshiped, and his greatest scheme is to tempt us to worship ourselves. But

Jesus shows us how to respond by quoting Deuteronomy 6:13 in Matthew 4:10: "Jesus said to him, 'Away from me, Satan! For it is written: 'Worship the LORD your God, and serve him only.'" This is where I want to live! Worship is life!

To further establish Satan's desire to be worshiped, listed below are several more verses:

> 2 Thessalonians 2:4 (speaking of the man of lawlessness): "He will oppose and will exalt himself over everything that is called God or is *worshiped*, so that he sets himself up in God's temple, proclaiming himself to be God."

> Revelation 13:4: "People *worshiped* the dragon because he had given authority to the beast, and they also *worshiped* the beast and asked, "Who is like the beast?"

> Revelation 13:12: "It exercised all the authority of the first beast on its behalf, and made the earth and its inhabitants *worship* the first beast, whose fatal wound had been healed."

> Revelation 13:14–15: "Because of the signs it was given power to perform on behalf of the first beast, it deceived the inhabitants of the earth. It ordered them to set up an image in honor of the beast that was wounded by the sword and yet

lived. The second beast was given power to give breath to the image of the first beast, so that the image could speak and cause all who refused to *worship* the image to be killed."

The scriptures make it very clear that Satan's desire is for worship, and he wants to destroy us by tempting us to worship ourselves – to do things our way instead of God's way. Misery loves company! I believe it is critically necessary to understand how Satan's desires and schemes are directly related to the battle for our worship. We are tempted through our own evil desires (James 1:14) to worship ourselves. But God will not give his glory to another or his praise to idols, so he calls us into a restored relationship with him through a life of worship – a life bowed down in adoration, reverence, and obedient service.

After all this battle talk, I think we are past due for some good news, so here is 1 Corinthians 15:57: "But thanks be to God! He gives us the victory through our LORD Jesus Christ." In light of eternity, we have the victory through Jesus Christ. This side of heaven, however, we are in a battle. We have been well equipped for this battle, and scripture is abundantly clear how to fight it. Why, then, does it seem to sneak up on us so easily, seemingly without notice? For that answer we will examine the two primary dynamics that are deeply ingrained in us and are at the heart of this battle: identity and security.

KEY POINTS

1. Our spiritual heart is in a constant posture of worship. We worship God or we worship the idol of self. God says he will not share his praise with idols. We are in a battle between worshiping God and worshiping self.

2. The three things we all have in common with Lucifer: a God-given design, a God-given position, and a God-given purpose.

3. We are constantly being tempted by our own evil desires and being lied to by our enemy to do things our way instead of God's way.

DISCUSSION QUESTIONS

1. What are your thoughts on the concept that the one true idol is self? (Exodus 20:3, 4 "make for *yourself...*" NIV; Proverbs 4:23; 1 John 5:21)

2. Discuss the description of Lucifer and his interaction with Eve and with Jesus. What similarities do you observe in humanity with regards to design, position, and purpose? (Ezekiel 28:11–17; Genesis 3:4, 5; Matthew 4:1–10)

3. How can you raise your awareness of the temptation to do things your way? What are some ideas or methods to fight this battle? (Matthew 6:9–13; Mark 14:38; Ephesians 6:10–18)

NOTES

CHAPTER 3

Identity and Security

"I have been crucified with Christ and I no longer live, but Christ lives in me. The life I live in the body, I live by faith in the Son of God, who loved me and gave himself for me."
Galatians 2:20

I was riding my bike a week after hearing the Holy Spirit of God speak into my thoughts the three messages I wrote about earlier, and I heard the breath of God repeating the phrase "I will not share my glory." Those words sounded familiar, and by searching a concordance I came to Isaiah 42:8: "I am the LORD; that is my name. I will not give my glory to another or my praise to idols." I knew this verse was to be part of the foundation upon which God was building our next season of ministry.

Over the summer months, the Holy Spirit began to speak a message to my heart, and I began to write it down. The message was a culmination of insights learned through the years of personal study and input from others, combined with the revelation of how certain pieces fit together. On Sunday, August 4, 2013, I delivered the message in all three of our morning services, which at the time was titled "A Vision for Corporate Worship." The

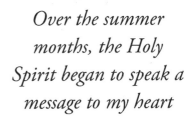

Over the summer months, the Holy Spirit began to speak a message to my heart

response was overwhelming, and we had a growing confidence that we were indeed walking in steps ordered by the Lord.

Over the next few weeks, I had the message sent out to several mentors and friends who were respected leaders from around the country. The response from each one of them was equally encouraging. Also during that time we began receiving written words of confirmation from many mature believers within our congregation. For months I read these daily and still refer back to them to this day.

During that same time we were thinking about what it would mean to possibly have a ministry built around preaching and teaching when our whole ministry lives had been on staff serving in the area of worship arts. Would we get a call from a church that wanted to partner with us in a way that would allow us to travel with this message? Would I be cold calling churches in hopes of finding opportunities to minister? While we had no idea what the future would hold, we began to consider ideas for a name for the ministry. We decided on *worship428*, which indicated the reference of the foundation verse from Isaiah and reflected the heart of the message: worship. Since then, we have been led to change the name of the ministry to *Worship Is Life*, which is reflected in the title of this book.

As the autumn months approached, our pastor gave us the freedom to explore opportunities to test the vision for the ministry. One evening in September, while walking on the treadmill, I felt impressed to contact the church where we spent our first years of ministry in the northeast suburbs of St. Paul, Minnesota, and ask about a potential weekend of ministry. As part of the weekend ministry, I also envisioned an accompanying workshop specifically designed for teams and leaders of corporate worship. It was suggested by a mentor of mine that we host a workshop on Long Island for area leaders and team members. Both of these events occurred in November 2013.

The first Saturday in November we hosted the workshop, where I delivered the message, presented the application for teams and leaders, and gave time for other experienced leaders to share input. We were blessed and encouraged by the responses of those who attended. On the third weekend of November, we traveled to the Twin Cities and ministered at Redeeming Love Church in Maplewood, Minnesota. I delivered the message during the Saturday evening service and then gave the workshop for team leaders and musicians. The next day I gave the message in both of the morning services. The pastor, our friend for nearly thirty years, was personally blessed and equally blessed us by proclaiming the weekend as a launching pad for the ministry. Many others who had watched us grow in our first years of ministry at Redeeming Love Church were deeply impacted by the message and poured out blessings of encouragement upon us.

That same weekend we also spent time looking at rental houses in the area with the help of a close friend who had become a real estate agent. During the summer months, we had a growing sense that if we were to relocate on our own it would be to the Twin Cities. This area represented our greatest networking potential for a new ministry. Attending college and serving at our first place of ministry in the Twin Cities area represented sixteen years of relationships with many leaders and friends who were still at the Assemblies of God university as well as at the MN Assemblies of God headquarters. We also had many friends from college who were pastoring in the surrounding area.

There is still much more to the story in those last couple of months before we left New York, but if it sounds like we were on a great journey riding off into the sunset to live happily ever after, that would only be partially true. We were on a great journey, and the Lord was confirming his word with signs of encouragement. However, I was not prepared for the battle I was about to face.

In chapter 2, I explained how scripture reveals Satan's greatest desire is to be worshiped, and his greatest scheme is to tempt us to worship ourselves. Scripture also reveals that Satan's primary weapon is lies. In fact, he is called the father of lies (John 8:44). He uses the weapon of lies to strike at the two areas that are central in the battle for our worship: identity and security. This is the true test of our relationship with God. Do we truly rest in who we

I was not prepared for the battle I was about to face

are in him? Do we actually trust him as our source? As I have battled through new levels of truly recognizing where I find my identity and place my security, I have become absolutely convinced this is where the battle for our worship rages.

Identity is linked to position and purpose, while security is linked to provision and possessions. Identity and security are also linked to each other.[1] In actuality they probably cannot be separated from each other, though it seems at times we feel

---

[1] I have been convinced of the spiritual significance of identity and security through study of the scriptures, personal experience, and observations of others. If you are interested in what secular psychologists say about this topic, you could search for Maslow's "hierarchy of needs" or psychologist Erik Erikson. Thank you to my first line editor and friend, Gary Lamm, for suggesting this note.

one more acutely than the other. While I believe identity is primary, when security is threatened it feels like it becomes primary. To see how these two dynamics are directly related to the battle for our worship, let us first revisit the accounts of Lucifer in the throne room with God, Lucifer in the garden with Eve, and Lucifer in the wilderness with Jesus.

We observed in the Ezekiel passage that God created Lucifer to be a covering cherub. God positioned Lucifer in the throne room for the purpose of covering, or guarding, God's presence. We are not told why it was necessary for this covering. Perhaps the necessity was for us to learn this crucial lesson from Lucifer's mistake. Lucifer chose to find his identity in his beauty and his splendor, resulting in his heart becoming lifted up and his wisdom becoming corrupted.

God was the source of Lucifer's beauty by creating him and positioning him. However, once Lucifer chose to find his identity in himself and not his God-given purpose and position, he became proud and was cast out of the presence of God. If this scenario sounds eerily familiar, it is. Maybe it is more familiar than we care to admit. Our natural tendency is to find our identity in who we are and what we do. Lucifer encourages this worldly pattern he first initiated by lying to us about our identity just as he lied to himself.

But what about Lucifer and security? What need did he have for provision and possessions? Provision and possessions are mostly related to a feeling of security about the future. Lucifer could not have asked for a more secure position. His future was eternally secure as long as he found his identity in his intended purpose and position. He forfeited his future security, his wisdom became corrupted, when he desired to raise up his position that he might be like the Most High. Since the beginning of mankind, Lucifer has attempted to deceive us in the same way he deceived himself.

When God made Adam and Eve, they were perfectly positioned in their identity. God made them in his own image (Genesis 1:27). He placed them in the Garden of Eden, where they enjoyed perfect relationship with him, with each other, and with creation. The Garden of Eden was not only a paradise for the body and soul; it accommodated the manifest presence of God. Adam and Eve walked and talked with God (Genesis 3:8–9).

Not only was their identity perfectly positioned by God, they were given purpose for living. "God blessed them and said to them, 'Be fruitful and increase in number; fill the earth and subdue it. Rule over the fish in the sea and the birds in the sky and over every living creature that moves on the ground'" (Genesis 1:28). "The Lord God took the man and put him in the Garden of Eden to work it and take care of it" (Genesis 2:15). "He brought them to the man to see what he would name them; and whatever the man called each living creature, that was its name. So the man gave names to all the livestock, the birds in the sky and all the wild animals" (Genesis 2:19–20).

Along with their identity being perfectly positioned and full of purpose, God blessed Adam and Eve with security through provision. They were given the provision of God's presence and the provision for physical sustenance: "Then God said, I give you every seed-bearing plant on the face of the whole earth and every tree that has fruit with seed in it. They will be yours for food" (Genesis 1:29). Talk about paradise. They had complete provision and yet none of their provision was dependent on their work. They worked simply for the fulfillment of their purpose while never giving a second thought to where their provision would come from. Like Lucifer, they lived in a state of perpetual security until they chose to look to themselves for their identity.

We see from the beginning how identity (purpose and position) is linked to security (provision and possessions). Lucifer tempts Eve by focusing on her identity (you will be like God), but he uses a source of provision (fruit from the tree of the knowledge of good and evil). This scheme is repeated countless times against all of humanity in the battle for our worship, and we witness it again in the temptation of Jesus.

Lucifer comes to Jesus and tempts him in the area of identity

Lucifer comes to Jesus and tempts him in the area of identity. The first two temptations both begin with "If you are the son of God ..." In other words, "Jesus, if you are who you say you are and who you think you are then turn these stones into bread or jump off the pinnacle of the temple." Take note of how provision is the source of the temptation. The first temptation involved bread, which is God's provision of food, just like the fruit with Eve. The second temptation involved the provision of God's protection: "throw yourself down. For it is written: 'He will command his angels concerning you, and they will lift you up in their hands, so that you will not strike your foot against a stone'" (Matthew 4:6). We can see the pattern Lucifer uses in tempting us to worship ourselves. He lies to us in regards to our identity and security. He will even use scripture to disguise the lie with a bit of truth.

As we were walking in obedience and following in the steps ordered by the Lord, I came under severe attack concerning my identity and security. My perspective of my relationship with God was being tested. I was thoroughly shocked to realize how much of my identity was wrapped up in what I do. While I knew this to be our tendency, especially as men, I had never been in a situation that so completely exposed the extent to which I was drawing my identity from the purpose and position of my work. As men we are tempted to find our identity in what we do and how important we feel. This dynamic is manifested in how important our position is, how much money we make, how strong or intelligent we are, and how good we are at what we do. While we were designed by God to *receive* a sense of *accomplishment* in what we do, we were never created to *strive* to find our identity in what we do (*fulfillment*).

In speaking to my wife and daughter, I have learned that women are tempted to find much of their identity in all things concerning appearance and relationships. We were definitely designed by God to receive a sense of *acceptance* in earthly relationships, but we were never created to *strive* to find our identity in earthly relationships (*fulfillment*).

While there is certainly some crossover between the primary areas men and women are tempted to find their identity, what men and women have in common is that this dynamic is fueled by the deadly act of comparison. In our twenty-first century media-driven world, the temptation to compare ourselves with others is intensified more than at any other time in history. Instead of comparing ourselves with the Joneses who live next

The moment you start comparing yourself to others is a warning sign you are finding your identity in yourself

door, the whole world is living in our house! The moment you start comparing yourself to others is a warning sign you are finding your identity in yourself.

Being removed from twenty-eight years of having the position of worship arts pastor, I was suddenly without a job. No longer could I find purpose in the daily routine of accomplishing the work I had become accustomed to doing. No longer was I recognized as the leader of corporate worship in a large congregation in New York. No longer was I the director, producer, conductor, and occasional singer and actor of seasonal productions that drew thousands of people each year. I was being bombarded by lies from the enemy that I was nothing. Never in my life was I more aware of the jobs of people around me. Everywhere I turned there was someone with a job, and I didn't have one.

And then there was security. Remember how security is tied to identity? Not only did I lack the purpose and position that seemingly comes with a job, I no longer had the provision and possessions that supposedly come from a regular paycheck. I was scared to death and at the same time felt like a big baby. I was hardly the first person to be in this situation, but it had been nearly thirty years since I was anywhere close to a similar position. By this point in my life, I should be providing ongoing stability for me and my family, right? What was I thinking packing up my family and all our belongings and moving halfway across the country to start a way of life normally reserved for missionaries, evangelists, and itinerant ministers? To be honest, there are days I still ask myself those questions. But on this journey of following the clear voice of the Holy Spirit of God, I have been led to new depths of finding my identity in Christ and placing my security in the hands of our Father.

In reality, when it comes to security, we are all in the same boat. Every person on the planet is completely dependent on God for his or her provision, but our tendency to place our security in other sources of provision causes us to feel insecure when those other sources dry up or disappear. We feel the weight of misplaced security more intensely when our circumstances position us in a place of need, and even more so if we don't see the answer coming around the corner. It is like dealing with the reality of death. We all live with the reality that we are going to die, but for most of our lives we don't give it much thought. However, if a person is on their deathbed or given a medical report indicating their days are numbered, the reality of death suddenly takes on a whole new perspective. Identity and security are challenged in ways we didn't know were possible. These are the times we are truly tested in where we are finding our identity and where we are placing our security. The enemy is armed and ready to launch an assault of lies to deceive us and cause us to fear. Thankfully we have God's Word as a primary weapon to fight this battle. Just as Jesus soundly rebuked the lies of Satan with the Word of God, we have the same powerful resource to gain victory in the battle for our worship.

A biblical-based understanding of sin is rebellion against God with self at the center. We are being constantly lied to by the enemy and tempted by our own evil

A biblical-based understanding of sin is rebellion against God with self at the center

desires to identify with Adam in his rebellion against God. But God invites us to turn away from identifying with Adam and turn toward identifying with Christ. "Therefore, if anyone is in Christ, he is a new creation, the old has gone, the new has come" (2 Corinthians 5:17).

Galatians 2:20 states: "I have been crucified with Christ and I no longer live, but Christ lives in me. The life I live in the body, I live by faith in the Son of God, who loved me and gave himself for me." As believers we find our identity in Christ. This is why water baptism is so important. Water baptism goes much deeper than affirming our public confession of Christ. Remembering our baptism reminds us we live each moment in the pattern of dying with Christ and rising with Christ – dead to self and alive to the Spirit. Worship is life!

As Christians, we find our identity in Christ and place our security in the hands of our loving heavenly Father. During this season I have spent much time abiding in Matthew chapter 6. For years the Lord's Prayer has been a part of my daily devotions, and "Give us today our daily bread" (Matthew 6:11) has taken on new meaning. Added to my prayers has been the "do not worry" section in Matthew 6:25–34. Jesus tells us not to worry about our basic needs because the Father already knows we need them. He has shown he will take care of us by his example of faithfully feeding the birds and clothing the lilies. Our part is this: "But seek first his kingdom and his righteousness" (Matthew 6:33a) and "Therefore do not worry about tomorrow" (Matthew 6:34a).

While a part of this journey has been battling through new levels of finding my identity and placing my security in God, I look back in wonder at the personal growth and miraculous provision that God has graciously given. I will share more about this in the final chapter. But first, let me share with you some thoughts about what it looks like to live a life of worship.

KEY POINTS

1. The two issues at the core of the battle for our worship are where we find our identity and where we place our security. God invites us to find both in him. Identity is linked to position and purpose, while security is linked to provision and possessions.

2. We were created to relate to others and to do work. We were not created to find our identity or security in earthly relationships or in the work we do.

3. Identity and security issues are intensified by comparing ourselves to others.

DISCUSSION QUESTIONS

1. What does it mean to find our identity and place our security in God? (Genesis 1:27–29; Psalm 18:32; Matthew 6:25–33; Galatians 2:20)

2. What are some of the areas in your life you have misplaced your identity and security?

3. Identify some of the ways you compare yourself to others.

NOTES

CHAPTER 4

Living a Life of Worship

"Do not conform any longer to the pattern of this world,
but be transformed by the renewing of your mind."
Romans 12:2a

I am glad you are still with me. Seriously, chapters 2 and 3 are a tough reality check. So let me start this chapter with the same good news that ended chapter 2. "But thanks be to God! He gives us the victory through our LORD Jesus Christ" (1 Corinthians 15:57).

I must confess that at first I did not want to write this chapter.[1] But *living* a life of worship is precisely where the *pattern* of worship meets the *purpose* of worship and the *pursuit* of worship. Still, I did not want to give the false impression that living a life of worship, our relationship with God, is reduced to following a list of rules. I must also

---

[1] Thank you to Dr. James Bradford for encouraging me with the necessity of writing this chapter.

confess that my personality type places a high value on my perception of what is right and on doing what is right. I could easily turn this chapter into a list of dos and don'ts and personally be quite content. However, this is not a contract, it's a covenant; a relationship. Still, every relationship has actions that are appropriate and actions that are inappropriate. It is no different with our relationship with God.

But finding that place of peace in our relationship with God often leads us to attempt to explain the unexplainable: *where the work of God* (revelation) **meets** *the work of man* (response). This point of discussion might possibly be the greatest source of theological debate throughout all history. You could argue that it is the primary reason for theological extremes, various world religions, numerous Christian denominations, and the anxiety many believers feel about their relationship with God on a weekly or even daily basis.

This struggle of finding the intersection where the work of God meets the work of man has been around since the "fall of man" because it is the result of the "fall." We see this struggle wrestled with in the scriptures by the likes of Paul and James.[2] Paul causes us to face the struggle again when he writes that salvation is by grace through faith, and not by works, so that we cannot take the credit. But, then he immediately writes that we were created to do good works (Ephesians 2:8–10). So, which is it? Well, I guess it's both. Then how much is God's part, and how much is my part?

---

[2] Romans chapters 3–7 and James 2:14–26.

Did I mention we are in a battle? I certainly don't claim to have the answers that are suddenly going to satisfy our logical understanding and emotional longing. To explain the unexplainable you would have to comprehend the One who is beyond comprehension, contain the One who is uncontainable, and describe the One who is indescribable. Instead of trying to do the impossible, I will share with you an insight about relationships that can give some perspective on where this struggle comes from.

We live in a world that teaches us that relationships are based on how *we* feel about the *other* person: *I* like you, *I* enjoy being around you, *I* love you, *I* don't like that person, *I* hate being around them, *I* don't love you anymore. If this sounds normal, but also self-centered, then you may want to sit down because it's about to get worse. When I first recognized this next part it practically knocked me over. Relationships that follow the pattern of the world, the pattern of self, are generally based on how the *other* person makes *us* feel about *ourselves*. You may want to read that again. This is the depth of the brokenness of our humanity.

If you haven't seen this before, I promise that if you do a little observing of yourself and others, it will become abundantly clear. You will see this reality attempt to play itself out in every relationship: from your pets, to the stranger on the street, to your family members, and especially your spouse. The more significant the relationship, the more it has the potential to come into play; which is precisely the point.

Since this perspective comes to us as naturally as breathing, we tend to take this approach into our most significant relationship; our relationship with God. We are inclined to base our relationship with God on *our* perception of how *he* makes *us* feel about *ourselves*. When my actions cause me to think that God feels good about me, then I feel good about myself. But, when I act in a way that makes me think that God doesn't feel good about me, then I feel bad about myself.

The focus on self not only wreaks havoc with our earthly relationships, it turns our relationship with God from a joy into a burden. So God, in his mercy, shows us how to do relationship. When God does relationship he doesn't focus on himself! He focuses on me, he focuses on you, and he focuses on others. Therefore, when I do relationship, God doesn't call me to focus on myself. He calls me to focus on him, to focus on you, and to focus on others. God does this through the pattern of revelation and response, and he calls this worship!

This is where the *pattern* of worship meets the *purpose* of worship. In chapter 1, I emphasized how God creates systems and has created a system to grow his kingdom; he works through those who are a part of his kingdom. As we focus on God by looking for him and listening for him, he is able to work through us to grow his kingdom as we respond to him and focus on others.

So how do we begin to describe a life of worship? Why is it so crucial that we look at life through the lens of worship? How can we be at peace with our understanding of where the work of God meets the work of man? The answers to these questions are exactly why we need to understand the biblical pattern of worship: God reveals, and we respond. This is where the *pattern* of worship meets the *pursuit* of worship.

For the sake of comparison, let's say the revelation of God, who he is and what he's done, is about 99.9 percent of the work, and our response is about .1 percent of the work. Our response is significant. After all, the covenant we enter into with God is a relationship. However, if we were to compare, our work of response pales in comparison to God's work of revelation. One of the main checkpoints I use in keeping the perspective of "where God's work meets our work" in a healthy tension is this: when I am getting my sense of spirituality from the work that I am doing, my heart is in the wrong place. Even this diagnosis is a challenge because "the heart is deceitful above all things" (Jeremiah 17:9), but it is an important starting point.

When we draw our sense of spirituality from the work we do, the result is spiritual pride, legalism, criticism, and a judgmental spirit

The work we do is a must, but it is not where we find our identity, place our security, or gain our sense of spirituality. When we draw our sense of spirituality from the work *we* do, the result is spiritual pride, legalism, criticism, and a judgmental spirit.

Our sense of spirituality is found in the revelation of the nature and work of God.

The pattern of revelation and response helps us better understand the relationship between grace, faith, and works. As mentioned earlier, Paul and James famously address this tug of war that we constantly find ourselves battling. After writing quite extensively about righteousness through faith in Romans chapters 3 and 4, Paul begins chapter 5 with these words:

> "Therefore, since we have been justified through faith, we have peace with God through our LORD Jesus Christ, through whom we have gained access by faith into this grace in which we now stand. And we rejoice in the hope of the glory of God" (Romans 5:1–2).

Without getting too hung up on the proper use of prepositions in attempting to describe the wonder of justification, we enter into a restored relationship with God through grace, by faith. It is easy to understand how grace is completely the work of God, but we tend to think that faith is completely the work that we do because there is an implied action on our part. However, faith is not only an action on our part but is an extension of God's grace. Paul writes about "the measure of faith God has given you" (Romans 12:3). Paul also shows us how faith is a foundational example of revelation and response: "Consequently, faith comes from hearing the message, and the message is heard through the word of Christ" (Romans 10:17).

So we're right back at trying to figure out another mystery; where does the work of God's grace meet the work of man's faith? We're also right back to our theological and doctrinal differences. For example, those who practice infant baptism tend to understate the work of man, and those who refer to believer's baptism as simply an ordinance (observing a rule), tend to overstate the work of man. I must admit, there are times I wish it was 100 percent the work of God and zero percent the work of me. This is simply not the case, as James so passionately tells us in chapter 2 of his epistle. To summarize: "so faith without deeds is dead" (James 2:26b). Relationship is a two way street.

Works are essential because the revelation of God requires a response. In the beginning of chapter 2, I pointed out that our response to the revelation of God can be favorable or unfavorable. We can have a favorable response to the revelation of God by bowing our lives to

Works are essential because the revelation of God requires a response

him, or we can have an unfavorable response to the revelation of God by bowing our lives to self. A favorable response is going to manifest itself through works. There is just no way around it. However, our perspective regarding works makes all the difference in the world.

Earlier I referred to a checkpoint in the struggle of grasping "where God's work meets our work." Another main checkpoint I use in keeping this perspective in a healthy balance is to remember the two things that happen when we initially respond favorably to the revelation of God. First, through the Spirit of God, we participate with Christ in communion with the Father. In other words, the revelation from the Holy Spirit of God invites us into a restored relationship with the Father made possible by the work of Christ and done in conjunction with Christ.[3] The focus point of redemption is not to escape hell and get into heaven, but rather the focus point of redemption is a restored relationship with Almighty God. This should be our motivation.

Second, through the Holy Spirit of God, we participate with Christ in his mission from the Father to the world.[4] This perspective is what helps the idea of works make sense. It speaks to our purpose as well as points back to our motivation. We don't do works to gain or maintain our righteousness.

---

[3] There are no words to adequately explain what we often refer to as the Trinity that can satisfy our finite, logical, and "enlightened" minds. I am in no way attempting to put God in a box or reduce him to a formula. "Hear, O Israel: The LORD our God is one" (Deuteronomy 6:4).

[4] I thoroughly resonated with the articulation of these two assertions made by James Torrance in his book *Worship, Community, and the Triune Grace of God.*

We do works because we have joined Christ in his mission to redeem the world. Even as I write this, I can once again sense the freedom that comes from this shift in motivation and purpose. I am not trying to prove myself to Christ. I am working with Christ in his mission! This is the response to the revelation of God I desire to have, and it deeply impacts how I interact with the world every moment of every day.

I am not trying to prove myself to Christ. I am working with Christ in his mission!

Now with the help of the Spirit and the Word, let's examine what it looks like to live a life of worship. If you have been a follower of Christ for any significant amount of time, do not expect to hear much, if anything, that sounds new. What is to follow could still sound like a list of dos and don'ts, but I trust it will sound different this time as you keep four things in perspective.

First, instead of thinking in terms of dos and don'ts, think in terms of revelation and response (relationship). Second, keep in mind that our spiritual heart is always in a posture of worshiping someone – God or self. Third, remember we are in a battle for our worship. Satan continually lies to us about our identity and security. While we have a new nature, we still war against the flesh and the desire to please ourselves. Fourth, the motivation is partnering with Christ in his mission to the world.

I explained in chapter 1 how the entire book of Romans follows the pattern of revelation and response. Romans chapters 1 through 8 are primarily revelation as Paul reveals the nature of God, and tells the story of God from creation to the future glory. After sharing about his heart for the Jews and his call to the Gentiles in chapters 9 through 11, Paul ends chapter 11 with his personal response and begins chapter 12 by urging us to respond by offering God our whole selves as living sacrifices. Then in verse 2 of Romans chapter 12, he begins his practical explanation of what this life response looks like:

> "Do not conform any longer to the pattern of this world, but be transformed by the renewing of your mind. Then you will be able to test and approve what God's will is – his good, pleasing and perfect will."

God works in patterns, and so it should not surprise us that the world has a pattern; to focus on self. Paul's first exhortation in living a life of worship is to live in accordance with God's pattern and not the pattern of this world, and be transformed by the renewing of our minds. The Greek word for the verb "be transformed" is in the present passive imperative form. Simply put, imperative means that it is a command, but passive means the action is done to us by someone else. The action of transformation is *done* by the Spirit and the Word, but our response is to *allow* the transformation to happen. Here again we see the work of God meeting our work. The verb form is also present, which in the Greek means this transformation is happening continually.[5] It falls on each one of us to continually allow the Spirit and the Word to reveal the areas to us where our tendency is to follow the pattern of the world: those areas that are manifestations of the idol of self.

I shared with you in chapter 1 how I wrestled with the world's pattern regarding sports. Two other areas I have had to wrestle down are television and finances. I have ups and downs in this wrestling match, but the reality is that the Spirit and the Word have revealed to me what I need to do in these areas. My part is to guard my heart and trust in God. It falls to me to respond in obedience with the help of the Holy Spirit of God. Here is where it gets easy to feel like it's more about my works than my faith through grace. That feeling is simply the enemy lying to me about where I find my identity and where I place my security.

Paul then goes on from Romans 12:2 through chapter 15 to lay out a lengthy list of dos and don'ts in this response

---

[5] Thank you to Mark Chaplin, lead pastor of Calvary Temple AG in Spearfish, SD, who encouraged me to study the Greek verb form of "be transformed" after I taught a "Worship Is Life" workshop for his leaders and musicians.

of living a life of worship. Here is just a partial list: do not think of yourself more highly than you ought, use the gifts you have been given to serve the body of Christ, hate what is evil and cling to what is good, practice hospitality, bless those who persecute you, live at peace with everyone, submit to governing authorities, love your neighbor as yourself, put aside the deeds of darkness, do not think about how to gratify the desires of the sinful nature, do not judge on disputable matters, make every effort to do what leads to peace, and bear with the failings of the weak.

Wow! After reading that list, how could you not feel like you are in the category of the weak? That's okay; we all are. That is why the power of God's grace is made perfect in our weakness (2 Corinthians 12:9), also written by Paul. If you feel yourself getting sucked back into feeling the weight of rules and regulations, go back and read the four perspectives that can help us see and hear these things in a way that not only makes sense but brings liberty. This is not a contract, it's a covenant; a relationship. While keeping a selfless perspective on our part can be challenging, it doesn't negate the reality that we have a part. To illustrate, I have included the visual of the stool from chapter 1, and included a look at what happens when the aspect of obedience is broken.

God's Pattern For Worship

REVELATION AND RESPONSE

WHO HE IS-REVERENCE

WHAT HE HAS DONE-ADORATION

WHAT HE SAYS TO DO-OBEDIENCE

WORSHiP iS
L i F E

God's Pattern For Worship

REVELATION AND RESPONSE

WHO HE IS-REVERENCE

WHAT HE HAS DONE-ADORATION

WHAT HE SAYS TO DO-OBEDIENCE

WORSHiP iS
L i F E

God describes worship the same way he describes relationship. Our relationship with him includes the response of obedience. It is a lifelong journey, but the beautiful thing is, as we obey, we are growing his kingdom!

I wanted to start by giving you this list from Romans because the whole book is such a beautiful pattern of revelation and response. Now I am going to give you some other checkpoints that are a part of a mind-set and attitude that reflects a life of worship.

One significant checkpoint is an attitude of thanksgiving and praise versus an attitude of complaining and grumbling. A life of worship is going to be expressed through a life of thankfulness. When we find ourselves complaining, it is a sure sign that the posture of our spiritual heart is turned toward self, and not God – unless, of course, you are bringing your complaint before God and crying out

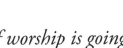

A life of worship is going to be expressed through a life of thankfulness

to him for mercy in times of trouble (Psalm 142:1–2). So many scriptures exhort us to give thanks and praise to God and warn us against complaining and grumbling. When we keep our eyes on God, our Creator and Redeemer, our response will naturally be thanksgiving and praise.

Another checkpoint has to do with where we put our hope and what we long for. Proverbs 13:12 says, "Hope deferred makes the heart sick." In other words, when we put our expectation or confidence in someone or something, and that expectation is delayed or removed, our thoughts and feelings become weak and wounded. A life of worship is expressed by putting expectation and confidence in God alone. Negative thoughts and feelings can be a blessing in disguise because they warn us that we are putting our hope in something, or someone, other than God.

The rest of Proverbs 13:12 says, "but a longing fulfilled is a tree of life." This part is a bit trickier to navigate. We can all relate to the feeling we get when something we have been longing for is fulfilled. This could be a short-term longing such as a food craving, your team winning the game, the weekend, payday, etc. Or it could be a long-term longing such as a promotion, your team winning the championship, vacation, a relational breakthrough, etc. When these earthly longings are fulfilled, it feels great! The challenge for us is that a longing fulfilled has the same euphoric feeling (tree of life) whether it is a worldly longing or a heavenly one. So how do we trust our heart to know the difference? All I can say is that as I have studied and endeavored to practice living a worshipful life, one of my daily prayers has become, "Almighty God, I long for your presence, your purpose, and your power. May your kingdom come and your will be done.

I put my hope in you alone. My identity is in you and my security is in you."

The next checkpoint refers back to the reality that, as believers, through the Holy Spirit we have joined Christ in his mission to redeem the world. My goal is to always have this in my mind as I am ministering to the church and interacting with the world. Every person has a story, is on a journey, and is in a battle of life and death for his or her worship. Consequently, I like to think in terms of being called as an armor bearer to come alongside people and help them fight their battles. I endeavor to keep this in mind whether I am leading a corporate worship service or interacting with the waiter at a restaurant. This could be as simple as interjecting an exhortation during a song to help refocus the attention of someone who may have become distracted from his or her worship, or asking the waiter if there is some need he has that we can pray for while we bless our food. A life of worship is partnering with Christ, through the Holy Spirit, to touch the Father's world.

The most effective checkpoint of all is the fruit of the Spirit. Most Christians are very familiar with Galatians 5:22–23: "But the fruit of the Spirit is love, joy, peace, patience, kindness, goodness, faithfulness, gentleness and self-control." When these attributes of the Spirit of God are evident in my life, it is a clear indicator of living a worshipful life. Conversely, when I am unloving, impatient, unkind, etc., it is a sure sign that I am serving the idol of self.

Living a life of worship is defined by Paul in Romans 8 as living according to the Spirit. As believers, we have the Spirit of God living in us, through us, around us, upon us, with us, and just about any other preposition you can think of. A frequent prayer of mine is: "Holy Spirit of God, help me be more aware of your presence, listening for your voice, bearing your fruit, and walking in your gifts." Notice how each part of the prayer has a part that the Spirit does and a part that I do. I can't tell you exactly where my part meets the Spirit's part, but I know that his part is by far the greatest, and yet it takes me doing my part. As the Spirit of God reveals, I am called to respond. Even in my response, the Spirit is helping me. Yes, God is beyond amazing!

I want to summarize all of this by sharing a phrase I believe the LORD has given me to help me in this lifelong journey. The phrase is 'living in awe of God'. 'Living' denotes a continuous state of being, and 'awe' indicates a posture of worship. I have developed an acrostic from the word 'AWE' to help me be more intentional in living the pattern of revelation and response: *Acknowledge, Welcome,* and *Engage.* I acknowledge who God has revealed himself to be. I welcome, or come into agreement with, what God has done. I engage by looking for him, listening for him, and responding to him throughout each day. I have a lot of room for growth, but I can confidently say that I am growing. As I grow, so does God's kingdom!

This practice is not a formula or an exact science, nor can we manipulate how and when God reveals himself. But there is a direct *relationship* between our level of engagement and the level by which God works through us. This is another one of God's patterns. Work produces results. But when we engage with work independent of God, what is produced will eventually perish (moth and rust and thieves; Matthew 6:19). When we engage with God, engage with work dependent on God, we grow his kingdom and what is produced lasts forever (the Son can only DO what he SEES the Father doing; John 5:19)!

The scriptures are full of checkpoints for living a life of worship, but I will conclude by making an application to our corporate worship. As believers who are called to daily live worshipful lives, we are also called to come together and worship corporately. There is a twofold purpose for these gatherings. The first is that we might glorify our God together. The second is to edify the church – to be built up and strengthened in order to grow God's kingdom (I Corinthians 14:26; Hebrews 10:24–25; 1 Peter 2:5, 9).

For both of these purposes to be fulfilled, one of the ways we do our part is by guarding our own mind-set, attitude, and motivation in regard to corporate worship. This is part of the battle. If we come to corporate worship with the attitude of "what is in it for me" or "what will I get out of it," then we are coming with the wrong perspective and for the wrong reason. Instead, the biblical perspective is that we gather for God, for one another, and for the world. The wonder is that when we come with the proper perspective, then our own life of worship is strengthened to stand strong in this world and to touch this world.

If we come with the wrong perspective, then the focus is on ourselves. When the focus is on ourselves, then all the opinions we have about the music, the preaching, the building, the leadership, the people, the finances, etc., turn into attitudes that completely derail the purposes for which we have gathered. There is no need to focus on ourselves because God is focused on us! We are all unique individuals, and we are going to have our opinions, but when it comes to our corporate worship, let's leave our personal preferences at the door and enter in with the Body of Christ to worship Almighty God together so that he will be glorified and we can be strengthened to go out and touch the world!

when it comes to our corporate worship, let's leave our personal preferences at the door

"Worship stands at the center of our purpose as God's people. We are his temple and his priests."[6] We

are his temple; we are where the Spirit of God dwells. We are his priests; we are the ones who serve him. With the help of God's Holy Spirit who dwells in us, we serve God by serving our family, our congregation, our community, and our world. Worship is life!

---

[6] This quotation is found in the introduction for 1 Peter in the *NIV Worship Bible.*

KEY POINTS

1. Finding peace in our relationship with God is directly linked to our struggle of trying to find the intersection of where the work of God meets the work of man.

2. Relationships that follow the pattern of the world, the pattern of self, are actually based on how the *other* person makes *us* feel about *ourselves*. We are inclined to base our relationship with God on our perception of how *he* makes *us* feel about *ourselves*.

3. God does not call us to focus on ourselves. He calls us to focus on him, and to focus on others. As we focus on God, he is able to work through us to grow his kingdom as we respond to him and focus on others.

4. The work we do is essential, but it is not where we find our identity, place our security, or gain our sense of spirituality.

5. We don't do works to gain or maintain our righteousness. We obediently serve because we have joined Christ in his mission to redeem the world.

6. A life of worship is going to be expressed through a life of thankfulness as opposed to complaining.

7. A life of worship is demonstrated by putting expectation and confidence (hope) in God alone.

8. When the fruit of the Spirit of God is evident in your life, it is a clear indicator of living a worshipful life.

9. Living in AWE of God: Acknowledge, Welcome, Engage. There is a direct relationship between our level of engagement and the level by which God works through us.

10. We help protect the purposes of corporate worship by guarding our own mind-set, attitude, and motivation.

DISCUSSION QUESTIONS

1. Discuss the age-old struggle of finding the intersection of where the work of God meets the work of man. (Ephesians 2:8–-10; James 2:14–26)

2. How can recognizing the perspective that the world's pattern for relationship is based on how others make us feel about ourselves help us be more selfless in our relationships? (Philippians 2:1–8)

3. List some examples of focusing on God and others in your family, congregation, and community.

4. With regards to doing work, discuss the distinction between *receiving* a sense of *accomplishment* (properly placed identity), and *striving* for a sense of *fulfillment* (misplaced identity).

5. What are examples of how your daily living can work with Christ in his mission to redeem the world? (2 Timothy 3:16, 17)

6. How does living out of a heart of thanksgiving, instead of complaining, help grow God's kingdom? (Philippians 4:6)

7. Discuss the various areas of life in which we are tempted to place our hope. What does it mean to place our hope in God in these areas? (Psalm 33:20–22; 42:11; 62:5, 6)

8. How does bearing the fruit of God's Spirit grow his kingdom? (Galatians 5:22, 23)

9. Identify ways you can raise the level of intentionally acknowledging, welcoming, and engaging God?

10. Discuss examples of guarding our mind-set, attitude, and motivation that may help protect the purposes of corporate worship.

NOTES

CHAPTER 5

A Vision for Corporate Worship

"What then shall we say brothers and sisters?
When you come together, everyone has a hymn,
or a word of instruction, a revelation, a tongue
or interpretation. All of these must be done
for the strengthening of the church."
1 Corinthians 14:26

Scripture makes it clear that biblical worship is a way of life that serves a purpose far beyond just ourselves; it is to grow God's kingdom. We also see in the scriptures that worship is an event, a corporate gathering which serves the same purpose by forming us to live a life of worship.

So, let me say first what corporate worship is not. Corporate worship is not coming as individuals to give our weekly worship to God. We are called to daily live out worshipful lives, and then we are called to gather and worship the Lord together. Something special happens when we gather to worship the Lord together. In fact, something supernatural happens when we gather together to worship the Lord. Something happens when we gather that doesn't happen when we don't!

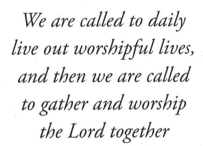

We are called to daily live out worshipful lives, and then we are called to gather and worship the Lord together

This chapter will be beneficial to all, but the content will be directed toward pastors and other church leaders for consideration when planning and leading corporate worship.

Pastors and Church Leaders

I am one of you. Just like you, I have a desire for God to be glorified, the church to be edified, and the people of the world to be reached. We have given our lives for the purpose of helping people connect their relationship to God to their relationship to life. Therefore, it is vital that we are keenly aware of the powerful reality that what we say and what we do, over and over again, forms us and forms the people.

More than anyone, we are probably the most aware of the battle we are in, but I don't know how many of us think of this battle in terms of worship. In fact, by the language we use, most of us have likely played a part in perpetuating the perspective people have today about worship. The language of today's church has formed us to look at worship through the lens of music and songs. There is no denying that music is a beautiful and powerful gift from God to accompany our worship and the work of God's Spirit. However, if we only use the word *worship* to refer to the music and those who are leading the songs, we actually encourage a narrow view of biblical worship. The result can be a dangerous disconnect between an act of worship and a life of worship, potentially hindering the growth of God's kingdom.

The language of today's church has formed us to look at worship through the lens of music and songs

As spiritual leaders, we desire for those we are leading to be in a relationship with God that fills every part of their lives. Looking at life through the lens of biblical worship is transformational in helping others understand the extent of what it means to have a relationship with God. We see clearly in the scriptures how God feels when our life of worship is not connected to our expressions of worship.

Proverbs 21:3: "To do what is right and just is more acceptable to the LORD than sacrifice."

Isaiah 1:13–16: "Stop bringing meaningless offerings! Your incense is detestable to me. New Moons, Sabbaths and convocations – I cannot bear your worthless assemblies. Your New Moon feasts and your appointed festivals I hate with all my being. They have become a burden to me; I am weary of bearing them. When you spread out your hands in prayer, I hide my eyes from you; even when you offer many prayers, I am not listening. Your hands are full of blood! Wash and make yourselves clean. Take your evil deeds out of my sight; stop doing wrong."

Isaiah 29:13: "The LORD says: 'These people come near to me with their mouth and honor me with their lips, but their hearts are far from me. Their worship of me is based merely on human rules they have been taught.'"

Jeremiah 7:9–11: "Will you steal and murder, commit adultery and perjury, burn incense to Baal and follow other gods you have not known, and then come and stand before me in this house, which bears my Name, and say, 'We are safe' – safe to do all these detestable things? Has this house, which bears my Name, become a den of robbers to you? But I have been watching! declares the LORD."

Hosea 6:6: "For I desire mercy, not sacrifice, and acknowledgment of God rather than burnt offerings."

Amos 5:21–24: "I hate, I despise your religious festivals; your assemblies are a stench to me. Even though you bring me burnt offerings and grain offerings, I will not accept them. Though you bring choice fellowship offerings, I will have no regard for them. Away with the noise of your songs! I will not listen to the music of your harps. But let justice roll on like a river, righteousness like a never-failing stream!"

Micah 6:6–8: "With what shall I come before the LORD and bow down before the exalted God? Shall I come before him with burnt offerings, with calves a year old? Will the LORD be pleased with thousands of rams, with ten thousand rivers of olive oil? Shall I offer my firstborn for my transgression, the fruit of my body for the sin of my soul? He has shown you, O mortal, what is good. And what does the LORD require of you? To act justly and to love mercy and to walk humbly with your God." (The word translated here as *mercy* refers to living in faithful, obedient relationship with God.)

Matthew 7:26–27: "But everyone who hears these words of mine and does not put them into practice is like a foolish man who built his house on sand. The rain came down, the streams rose, and the winds blew and beat against that house, and it fell with a great crash."

Matthew 15:8–9: (Jesus quoting Isaiah) "These people honor me with their lips, but their hearts are far from me. They worship me in vain; their teachings are merely human rules."

What is our role as leaders in guarding against empty sacrifices? How do we help those we are leading in our corporate gatherings make a better connection in their relationship to God and their relationship to life? This is a challenging tension, where on the one hand we certainly

we are called as leaders to partner with the Holy Spirit in pointing to the revelation of God and encouraging the people to respond

don't control the Spirit of God or the hearts of the people, nor are we called to whip the people into a frenzy or to beat them down into submission. On the other hand, we are called as leaders to partner with the Holy Spirit in pointing to the revelation of God and encouraging the people to respond.

I am convinced that the key is to approach our corporate gatherings with an intentional and consistent approach of following the biblical pattern of worship: revelation first and then response. The biblical pattern of revelation and response transcends time, location, race, culture, age, style, denomination, you name it.

In chapter 1 we did an extensive, though hardly exhaustive, study of the biblical pattern of revelation and response. How do we take this pattern and apply it to our corporate worship? I believe Christian gatherings of all kinds would do well to teach, follow, and emphasize this pattern, but I want to take some time to address the model found in most Pentecostal and Evangelical settings.

The current model in these gatherings generally follows the pattern of songs, sermon, short response, and "Come back next week!" Somewhere in there we receive an offering. This is the model I was raised in, trained in, and ministered in for most of my twenty-eight years as a worship arts pastor. While many of you may know the history of this model, others may not. I want to briefly share some of the history and more recent developments that have led us to where we are in many of our services today.

Now I am in no way suggesting that we as Pentecostals and Evangelicals throw away our model and start from scratch. Rest assured, the pattern is happening when you gather. I am suggesting we take a serious look at where we have come from and ask ourselves how we can be more intentional as we infuse our current model with the biblical pattern of revelation and response.

The Reformation of the 1500s brought an emphasis on the Word of God and a rebirth of preaching. Also with the Reformation came an explosion of denominations as various leaders found their voices in the midst of not only the changes in worship within the church, but also the changes in how society viewed God as a result of the Enlightenment – the age of reason and logic. As these changes moved west to America followed by settlers moving farther west, a new pattern developed, which we identify as the revival meeting movement. The long established model of a community gathering to worship God changed to an intense desire to see individual conversions now that people required being convinced of their need of God in a world of rationale. This movement was led by the likes of Charles Finney and D. L. Moody. One of the primary means these evangelists used to draw crowds was to direct their music leaders to use the music style of the times to bring people in. Sound familiar? We have not ventured far from this approach.[1]

---

[1] One of the places you can read about this part of our history is *Twenty Centuries of Christian Worship*, edited by Robert E. Webber.

Now add to this model the Church Growth Movement that began in the 1960s, which uses societal factors to attract people – the most dominant one being music. Then add the commercialization of Christian worship music and now immediate access to countless songs as well as Internet exposure to popular worship groups from around the world, and it is no wonder that our idea of worship is so heavily driven by music.[2]

I am not at all trying to give music a bum rap. As I stated earlier, music is a beautiful and powerful gift from God to accompany our worship and the work of the Spirit of God. Toward the end of this chapter, I will share the main reason why music and songs are so powerful in our understanding of worship. But music doesn't do worship, nor does it do the work of the Spirit of God. Songs can inspire us, teach us, help us lift our voices as one voice to declare our beliefs and express our praise and adoration of God, but the presence of music does not guarantee any of these things are truly happening. We live in a world that is constantly critiquing and applauding musical talent and presentations. So music can also be a snare. God designed music to help get our attention on him, but Satan will use music to get our attention on ourselves. How else can you explain that the music that so beautifully accompanies our worship is the same music that causes strife and division in the church?

---

[2] Some of these thoughts were solidified in conversations with Dr. Dave Collins, my supervisor during my internship for my master's in worship studies.

Music is personal. With the increased exposure to different styles of music and the increased emphasis on individuality, mixed with the ancient battle of self-worship, music domination in corporate worship has tremendous potential to derail the purpose for which we come together: to glorify God and to strengthen the church to touch the world. We cannot assume at all that having a group of musicians lead songs in a quality way with sincere hearts means we are fulfilling the purpose for which we are gathering.

This truth is dramatically illustrated when David is attempting to bring the Ark of the Covenant into Jerusalem (2 Samuel 6 and 1 Chronicles 15). The first time David was moving the Ark, he assembled the singers, the musicians, and came with a sincere heart and an unrestrained personal response. But it ended in disaster because he had not consulted the LORD on how to move the Ark. He led out of response instead of leading out of revelation. After inquiring of the LORD how the Ark was to be moved, he brought the same response and there was tremendous joy and a great celebration!

So what exactly am I suggesting? We know that we cannot force anyone to have a worshiping heart. The mystery of revelation is that it comes by the Spirit and

The mystery of revelation is that it comes by the Spirit and the Word working together

the Word working together. It is impossible to separate the two for they are *one*. The singing time is not intended to be exclusively for God's Spirit to work, any more than the preaching time is intended to be exclusively for God's Word to work. Pentecostals have been accused of being strong in Spirit but weak in Word, while Evangelicals have been accused of being strong in Word but weak in Spirit. God's Spirit and his Word cannot be separated! *God is One*! Oh the mystery of God!

I have shared with you my *theology* of worship in regard to revelation and response. My *philosophy* of leading worship is that we partner with the Spirit of God to emphasize the wonder of who God is and what he has done, and then encourage a response. This philosophy carries over into the *implementation* of corporate worship as well as ministering to others through a life of worship. Let me share some examples of implementing revelation and response in our corporate worship.

Because of the working of God's Spirit, his Word not only says something, but it also does something. With this in mind, a great place to start for the focus point of a given service is to allow the gathering to be directed by the revelation the appointed speaker has been given by the Spirit of God. Most often this appointed speaker is going to be the lead pastor. Most congregations function with the lead pastor being the one called by God to lead a given congregation for a given period of time. This pastor has a mandate and responsibility to bring the revelation of God to the people. The revelation from the Word, by the Spirit of God, becomes the directive for the service.[3]

Shaping the service around this revelation goes deeper than just being thematic. In terms of music, the idea is not to run out and find a group of songs that fit the theme of the message, but knowing the focus point of revelation will assist tremendously in the mysterious process of the Spirit of God directing others who will give leadership in the corporate worship. This includes scriptures to be used in other places of the service to support the sermon, songs that will be sung, prayers that will be prayed, and transitional statements that will be made. It's not a formula; it is a pattern that can be followed in countless creative ways: the biblical pattern of revelation and response.

Now I realize that not every speaking pastor has the message prepared far enough in advance for this kind of planning, and that's fine. The Holy Spirit of God has all the ability necessary to do his work through and by his Word. Regardless of the model of service or the extent of planning, our part is to be mindful and intentional about following the biblical pattern Almighty God has set forth.

Whether our role is preparing and leading the singing worship, the praying worship, the giving worship, etc., the safest place to lead from is following the biblical pattern of

---

[3] For a thorough unpacking of how a scripture-directed approach can impact a congregation, I highly recommend the book *Preaching as Worship*, by Michael J. Quicke.

revelation and response. In the opening chapter, I referenced the two primary biblical principles of revelation. The first one is the nature and work of God as Father, Son, and Holy Spirit of God. The second is God's story: creation, the fall of mankind, Christ's redemption, Christ's resurrection, life through the Spirit, Christ's return, and eternity.

Since many of us follow a corporate worship model that includes a significant amount of songs and singing, I will use this element of worship as an example. Songs that we sing in our corporate worship have lyrics that reflect revelation and response. I think the best songs are those that begin with revelation and invite response. Some songs are entirely revelation, while some are entirely response. The key is first recognizing and then emphasizing, or pointing to revelation, and then encouraging response. Keeping in mind that the pattern is revelation first, if the opening song is primarily response, I am going to be mindful of starting with a scripture or a short word of testimony that will point to a revelation of God and inspire the response that the song is encouraging.

For example, the song "Come, Now Is the Time to Worship" is a song that is entirely response.[4] If I were to use this as an opening song, I would point to the revelation of God by starting with Philippians 2:10–11: "that at the name of Jesus every knee should bow, of those in heaven, and of those on earth, and of those under the earth, and that every tongue should confess that Jesus Christ is LORD, to the

---

[4] "Come, Now Is the Time to Worship," by Brian Doerksen.

glory of God the Father." This is the scripture that inspired the song, but now I have emphasized and pointed to the revelation that Jesus Christ is Lord to the glory of the Father and is worthy of our worship and praise! This may seem subtle, but, believe me, it is profound for the response of the people. Instead of sending the message that we start with our response, we communicate that we are responding to the revelation of God, the initiator. In addition, the people will know that when they sing verse 1 of the song, they are singing the Word of God!

Scripture verses can be implemented during the flow of songs in a variety of ways. They can be declared by a pastor or another leader, lay person, teenager, or child. The leader can invite the people to repeat certain phrases. The verse or verses can be displayed on a screen, and the people could be invited to declare them. Certain words, phrases, or sections can be highlighted in a different color, and they can be instructed to declare those parts. I have witnessed time and time again how enthusiastically the people respond when they are declaring scripture together. How often do you think the average believer hears his or her own voice declaring scripture out loud? Remember, the Word and the Spirit work together!

While the Spirit-inspired scripture is the greatest source of revelation, we can partner with the Spirit of God by being aware of the points of revelation in the lyrics of the songs. During song introductions, instrumental interludes, and transitions between songs, we as leaders can emphasize these points through prayers, expressing worship, and transitional statements.

For example, the song "Great Are You Lord" has points of revelation in the verse, while the chorus and the bridge are responses.[5] During the introduction of the song, I would be verbally worshiping the Lord by emphasizing one or more points of revelation in the lyrics of the verse: "Lord, You are the One who gives us life," "You are the One who dispels the darkness with Your light," or "You are the One who restores our broken hearts."

This type of leadership not only points to the revelation of who God is, but also inspires people to respond. I used to struggle with the idea that I did not want to come across like a cheerleader trying to create a response from the people. That all changed when I began to see myself as an armor-bearer, one who comes alongside another to help him fight his battle. The battle for our worship does not stop when we gather to worship together. Distractions, worries, guilt, and other factors war against each person at some time or another during the course of a service. Our role as armor-bearers is to help people fight the battle for their worship. When they hear our voice as leaders speak out and point to the revelation of God or encourage a response, it helps to draw them in and engage their hearts for the purpose we have gathered.

I trust these examples are able to get you started in thinking about how to implement the biblical pattern of revelation and

---

[5] "Great Are You Lord," by All Sons and Daughters.

response. A theology and philosophy of worship that focuses on our response being primary is not going to stand up in times of trials, testing, and persecution. Leading corporate worship in a way that follows the pattern we find in scripture allows freedom for the Spirit and the Word to work together and strengthen the people to stand strong in this world and to touch this world!

This is how corporate worship forms our life of worship and intersects with the *purpose* and the *pursuit* of worship. In chapter 4, I shared with you the phrase 'living in AWE of God': Acknowledge, Welcome, and Engage. Here lies the reason why music and songs are so powerful in our worship. The mystery behind how God created us to respond to music, combined with the lyrics that reveal God and encourage us to respond, help bring us to a place of acknowledging, welcoming, and engaging! The songs help us become more aware of God as we resonate with his pattern of revelation and response. The purpose of our corporate worship is to form us to live a life of pursuing this pattern. Why? Because it is God's pattern for worship and it is how he grows his kingdom. He works through us who are a part of his kingdom. Worship is life!

KEY POINTS

1. Corporate worship is when we gather to worship God together.

2. What we say and do, over and over again, forms us and those we lead. When corporate worship follows God's pattern of revelation and response, it forms us to live a life of worship (relationship) by following his pattern.

3. Leaders cannot make revelation happen any more than they can make sincere response happen. However, leaders are called to partner with God to *emphasize revelation* and *encourage response.*

4. While we need to guard our hearts regarding music because we can make it so personal, it plays a powerful part in helping us to acknowledge, welcome, and engage God.

DISCUSSION QUESTIONS

1. What are some of the ways we can emphasize that our gathering is for worshiping God *together?* (Acts 2:42–47) (Ephesians 4:12, 13)

2. List some things that are currently said and done on a consistent basis in your service. Which of these sayings or actions are forming the people to live a life of worship? Which of these sayings or actions may have some unintended consequences?

3. Think about each element of the service. What are practical and creative ways the pattern of revelation and response could be implemented?

4. What are ways we can continue to incorporate music while emphasizing its role in forming us to acknowledge, welcome, and engage?

NOTES

CHAPTER 6

God's Provision

"Blessed rather are those who hear the
word of God and obey it."
Luke 11:28

With obedience, a life of worship, comes blessing; this is one of God's patterns. I would like to give testimony to this truth and share a few more personal stories from our journey over the last couple of years.

As the time was approaching for us to leave New York, a great concern was where we were going to live. We knew we were going to look for a place to rent, but we had no idea what our monthly income was going to be. We weren't leaving for a position that was going to be providing a regular paycheck, so we had no proof of income to show any rental company, and they were requiring verification of monthly income three times the amount of rent. We definitely needed a miraculous provision from God!

We began looking online at places for rent all over the Twin Cities area, knowing the best option for our family would be a single-family home because of all the live music that took place, especially with Taylor. Instruments like the piano, drums, and electric guitar, along with mixing in some vocals from time to time, might make us unwelcome neighbors in an apartment or attached townhouse community. After searching through dozens of rental homes online and looking at four or five places when we visited Minnesota in November (only two and a half months before leaving New York), we decided on a $300 difference between the minimum and maximum for monthly rent. We weren't thrilled about most of the places we were finding in our price range, especially those toward the lower end, but we were prepared to make adjustments in living style if it came down to that.

In the early stages of our house search we had been encouraged by some to stay away from Craigslist when it came to rentals. As the time was drawing close, about the middle of December, we were encouraged by a friend to take a look at Craigslist. He had quite a bit of experience in house rentals, so we thought there was no harm in looking. We punched in our price range for places with three bedrooms. As we were browsing the results, all of a sudden a picture of a beautiful two-story house popped up. I looked at the price and immediately thought, "Something is wrong with this picture." The price was a little above the halfway point of our range, but the house was significantly nicer looking on the outside than anything we had seen at the top of our range.

Most places we looked at online had twelve to twenty pictures posted, but this place only had five. Two of them were of the outside front, one in summer and one in winter, and three showed small snippets of the inside. Still thinking there must be something wrong with the place or there was a mistake in the price listing, I called the phone number. The gentleman who answered had a strong accent and was a little challenging to understand, which didn't help to ease my doubts. He said the previous renters had signed a three-year lease but were called to another state because of job relocation. One of the many prophetic words we received from our respected congregants was that the Lord was moving things around in preparation for our transition!

The owner said the house was in great shape and the rent was lower because it was more difficult to find renters in the winter. Later we learned that Woodbury, a growing suburb of St. Paul, had been overbuilt, and, for a time, both sale prices and rental prices were deflated. I asked him if our real estate agent friend, Becky, could come over and walk through the house, and he agreed. She called us immediately after the walk-through and told us we would love the place. A couple days later we had Becky and our daughter, Kelsie, meet with the owner. Kelsie then introduced us to the owner and walked us through the house using FaceTime. We loved it but remained cautious as we waited to see what the owner would make of our financial situation.

Becky explained to the owner that we were moving to the area to start a new endeavor and could not provide proof of income but would be willing to fax him our bank statements. She also told him she had known us for thirty years and vouched for our reliability. He agreed to take a look at the statements.

Meanwhile, this was the middle of December, and we were not arriving till February 2 and were hoping to not have to pay for January. He said, "No problem." If he was comfortable with the bank statements, he would hold the place for us, and we could even move in early if necessary! He said he had just turned down someone who had plenty of money but would not submit to background checks on all who would be living there, and he needed to know he would have good renters for his neighbors. We faxed him our bank statements and a few days later received the lease. Later we learned he was from China, was a Christian, and attended a Chinese church just around the corner. They have been wonderful landlords. We had a miraculous provision from God!

It was around the middle of December when I was speaking to Joe Anderson, lead pastor of Summit Church in St. Paul, where Kelsie and her husband, Ben, serve as worship leader and youth pastor. Joe had previously been on the road as an itinerant minister for three years, and it was during this conversation that he gave me one of several critical points of council. Joe said, "Todd, you need to gather some monthly support as you begin this ministry." I am a little embarrassed to say I had never even thought of this, but I knew immediately that he was right.

In a couple weeks our ministry team in New York was putting on an appreciation banquet for us. I asked our pastor if he would be willing to allow us to ask for monthly supporters that night. It was a beautiful evening that we will never forget as the choir sang, the orchestra played, memorable gifts were given, and I literally passed (handed) a baton to the incoming worship arts pastor. At the end of the evening I shared again about the mission the Lord was calling us to and invited them to consider supporting us on a monthly basis. That was the beginning of gathering ministry team members, family, and friends to help us move the vision forward. To this day, their support is a significant part of God's provision for us and our ministry.

Saturday, February 1, 2013, was the day for packing the trucks. Brenda had spent months sorting, selling, giving away, and packing. Thanks to her, when the day came, we were ready. We had over forty friends from our ministry team and congregation arrive at 9:00 a.m., and we were completely packed with the house cleaned by 1:00 p.m. They were amazing!

Another remarkable provision is connected to this part of the story. We had rented two trucks and a tow trailer. We had two different estimators calculate the needed space, and we thought we were in good shape with the large truck and one a little over half the size. We picked up the large truck a couple of days early because we had piano movers coming to load our two pianos. When I saw the space those two pianos took as they were positioned in the truck, I began to get nervous about having enough room.

On Friday we went to pick up the second truck. I knew it was obviously going to be significantly shorter in length than the large truck, but when we pulled up and saw it, I was stunned to see how small it was. Not only was it significantly shorter in height, but it extended over the cab, so the real length was two feet shorter than I was anticipating. I knew we were in trouble, and didn't know what to do. You needed to reserve these trucks days or weeks in advance, as this was a smaller place for pick up and drop off only.

As I pulled into the small parking lot, I noticed the top of a truck rising above the fenced-in area adjacent to the office. It was the same height as the large truck we already had at the house, but a few feet shorter in length. I said to Brenda that I thought it was the next size down, and we wondered about the chances of it being available. We walked in, and I asked the manager about the truck. He said it was the strangest thing. It was just dropped off that morning, and he had no idea that it was coming. I asked him if it would be available, and he said he just needed to check it in, fill it with fuel, and it was ours for the taking!

We were so glad it was. Even before we were through packing, I was getting nervous that all our belongings weren't going to fit in both trucks, and had visions of giving stuff away as our helpers were leaving. Our friends did a masterful job of packing. Both trucks were packed to capacity, and everything fit. I am not embarrassed to say I let out a victory shout! I knew without a doubt that the provision of that second truck was the sovereignty of God on display once again!

The next morning our caravan left at 6:00 a.m. A dense fog was covering the entire area. As we headed toward New York City, daylight arrived, and the fog began to lift. It was a sobering and yet comforting sign that mirrored what we were feeling; the future seemed enveloped with fog, but the Lord would light our path.

Our friend, Todd Luse, had graciously offered to drive the big truck, which was also towing our van. I followed with the next truck, and Brenda drove our car. Kelsie had flown out to help pack and drive. Taylor switched back and forth between vehicles. We drove fourteen hours on the first day and ten hours on the next. We had beautiful clear skies and roads the entire trip even though each state we traveled through was hit with a storm within hours of us passing through.

As we headed west, the farther we drove the colder it became and the deeper the snow cover. When we arrived in Woodbury on Monday evening, the temperature was zero degrees, and two and a half feet of snow was on the ground.

We had endured Minnesota winters when we lived there before, but I must admit, we were questioning the Lord's timing of this move.

Beyond the misery factor of the cold and snow, we had concerns about Taylor and his schooling. When we left New York, he had just finished the first semester of his sophomore year at our Christian school, where his entire class size was forty. When we arrived in Woodbury, he landed in the middle of a trimester at a public school where his class size was four hundred. We were amazed at the smooth transition. His classes worked out fine. His first day was on a Thursday, and by Friday night he was playing in the pep band at the girls basketball game. He also became immediately involved in the Bible club and appreciated the opportunity to have an influence in the setting of a public school for the first time. But this part of the story gets even better!

Minnesota has an education program called Post Secondary Enrollment Options (PSEO). It allows juniors and seniors in high school to enroll at participating colleges and universities and take classes that count for both high school and college credits. There is no cost for tuition, fees, or books, as long as the student is enrolled in high school. We knew this program existed, and our plan was to allow Taylor to decide if he felt he should participate in PSEO his junior year or wait for his senior year.

What we were not aware of at the time is that we needed to live in Minnesota for six months in order to become residents so he would be eligible. If we had not moved in February, Taylor would not have been allowed to participate in PSEO his junior year! Taylor did decide to participate, and for two years he attended North Central University (NCU), our alma mater, full time as a high school student. He graduated from high school, and at the time of this writing is a junior in college while having completed his freshman and sophomore years for the cost of transportation and a daily meal! In addition, the opportunities he has been given to grow in his giftings and calling have amazed us. The provision of God's timing is a tremendous blessing that comes with obedience.

Another area of concern was income. When we lived in New York, Brenda taught piano out of our home, and we were trying to figure out what avenues to take now that we were living in an area that we had left seventeen years ago. Building up an adequate number of students could be a real challenge. Several months before we moved, I had asked Larry Bach, dean of fine arts at NCU, if Brenda's teaching experience would qualify her to teach beginner and intermediate piano students at the university. He said yes, but there would have to be an opening, which at the time there was none. Four months after we moved here, we were at a wedding reception for Kelsie's sister-in-law. Larry was seated at the table next to us, and during the reception came over and asked Brenda, "How would you like to teach piano at NCU this year?" We were floored! Brenda is working at the university and loves teaching and mentoring her students! What a timely provision it has been!

There are so many more stories from our journey that testify to the Lord's blessing on our obedience to follow his leading: from being a ten-minute drive to Kelsie and Ben's and watching and helping their ministry, to unexpected checks in the mail, to being appointed the worship arts director for the MN Assemblies of God, to all the amazing opportunities we have had to minister in churches across the country and now around the world with my recent trip to Tanzania, Africa. God calls each one of us to lay our lives down before him, and accept his invitation into a relationship of worshipful obedience. Worship is life!

KEY POINTS

1. A life of worship involves obedience.

2. One of God's patterns is that blessing follows obedience.

DISCUSSION QUESTIONS

1. Recall moments and times of obedience (response) to God's direction (revelation).

2. Share stories of times you saw God's blessing follow your obedience.

NOTES

ACKNOWLEDGMENTS

"I thank my God every time I remember you."
Philippians 1:3

To God Almighty, who has revealed himself as Spirit, Creator, and Redeemer, who is perpetually reaching out to us and is faithfully there to help us. I am your beloved child and faithful servant, and I bow my life before you.

To Brenda, for partnering with me in life and ministry and for being a shining example of a wife, mother, and faithful servant of God.

To Kelsie and Taylor, you are the joy of our lives. We thank God for you and are blessed beyond measure to see his presence and purpose being fulfilled in each of you.

To Ben, thank you for being a loving and faithful husband to Kelsie and for all the help and encouragement you have been to me.

Thank you to all our family and friends who have loved and supported us through the years and, in particular, on this part of our journey.

To the pastors, staff, and congregations where we have served over the last three decades, thank you for pouring into us.

We are forever indebted to those who have supported us through prayer and giving as we have been commissioned by God to launch out into the deep with this ministry to touch his church and the world.

ABOUT THE AUTHOR

Todd Marshall is founder and president of Worship Is Life. This ministry strengthens the local church to touch its community by exhorting leaders, musicians, and congregations to minister in, and live out, the biblical pattern of worship: revelation and response.

Prior to launching this full-time ministry, Todd served as a worship arts pastor for thirty years. Graduating North Central University in 1985 with a BS in sacred music, he began his full-time ministry with Redeeming Love Church in the suburbs of St. Paul, Minnesota.

In 1997, Todd and his family moved to central Wisconsin, where he served the congregation of First Assembly of God in Plover. Three and a half years later, he transitioned to Smithtown, New York, on Long Island, and served for nearly fourteen years at Smithtown Gospel Tabernacle.

Marshall has been certified as a life coach and holds a master's degree in worship studies from the Institute for Worship Studies in Jacksonville, Florida.

Todd and his wife, Brenda, along with their son, Taylor, reside in Woodbury, Minnesota. Their daughter, Kelsie, is married to Ben Freitag. Kelsie and Ben serve as worship leader and youth pastor at Summit Church in St. Paul, Minnesota.

INTERESTED IN HOSTING
WORSHIP IS LIFE MINISTRY?

The vision of Worship Is Life is to strengthen the church's mission to reach the world by encouraging believers to say yes to a life of worship.

The implementation of this vision is primarily carried out through a weekend of ministry to a local congregation. Todd delivers the Worship Is Life message to the people and offers an accompanying workshop for pastors, leaders, and musicians that discusses infusing the pattern of biblical worship into the corporate gathering and life of the church. The vision can also be carried out through conferences, pastor's meetings, workshop-only events, and group or one-on-one coaching.

If you are interested in contacting Todd and Worship Is Life ministry, please visit www.worshipislife.org.